The Wolver Newport Pagnell Branch

by Bill Simpson

Lamplight Publications

Published by Lamplight Publications
260 Colwell Drive, Witney, Oxfordshire OX8 7LW
and 38 Spinney Drive, Cherwell Heights,
Banbury, Oxfordshire OX16 9TA

First published 1995

ISBN 1 899246 01 0

Printed and bound at the Alden Press, Oxford

Foreword

The accessibility of the motor car has reduced the value of travel as an experience. Distance means far less than it used to and many people travel many miles each day in the course of their daily work. The mind is now focussed totally on the destination and completing the journey.

In a travelling world of such scope booking a ticket to take a train ride of four miles appears almost an absurdity. It is highly unlikely, if it were still possible, that many would consider parking their car at Wolverton station to travel to Newport Pagnell. One could therefore, however reluctantly, conclude that the closure notice instigated by the notorious Dr Beeching has been finally vindicated. How appropriate it would have been had the branch achieved its early objective of reaching Olney and Wellinborough must remain the stuff of historical conjecture.

All that being said the branch was far from ineffective and provided a very valuable role from its first trains, bringing the workmen to and from industrial settlements that grew along the line at Bradwell and Great Linford besides Newport Pagnell and surrounding districts to Wolverton Carriage Works. Daily timetables show a regular intensity of traffic, eleven return trains in the 1880's, more than twelve trains each way in the late 1930's Even up to closure in 1964 a regular eight trains each way.

This book is intended as a study of a branch line set against the mighty edifice of the Works. The 'Newport Nobby' became part of the folklore of the district, a reassuring sense of permanence and reliability. Bringing the community together each day if only for eleven or twelve minutes, a need that is never outmoded.

Bill Simpson, 1995

Wolverton from Blue Bridge. The original London & Birmingham route can be seen on the extreme left whilst the avoiding route of 1882 is on the right, between them is the bulk of the works and the 'up' sidings. Beneath the connecting line on the bridge from the 'down' slow is the is the burrowing junction line connection with the 'up' slow. The signal box is Wolverton No. 1.

Bob Ayres Collection.

CHAPTER ONE

Newport Pagnell

The town of Newport Pagnell had something of a struggle to get the communications it needed. After a very good start in the coaching age with 188 road services per week from ponderous wagons with six heavy horses shackled to the front to speedy mails and stagecoaches of which there were 33 in 24 hours.

It had to work hard to maintain organised transport links first with the canal system and secondly with the railways. Milton Keynes and the M1 Motorway have now brought the story full circle, back to the road.

The Grand Junction Canal from Brentford to Braunston was intended as a relief waterway to the well used Oxford Canal (1770) and was opened throughout in 1805.

Wending its way the canal passed through Linford and continued north close to the old village of Wolverton which was half a mile or so west of the industrial development that followed bearing its name.

With the opening of the canal Newport Pagnell had at least the prospect of a connection over a short distance of 1¼ miles to Linford. Like the many railway promotions of the later years the canal was initiated with the grander prospect of connection between the Midlands and East Anglia.

To this effect a connection with the Newport Pagnell Canal Co received The Royal Assent in 1814. The Canal was opened in January 1817, the year that the Kilmarnok & Troon Railway was first worked by a steam locomotive. In ten years the golden era of the canal age would have to assert itself to the prospect of the end of its monopoly. Nevertheless, at a place west of Newport town called 'The Green' a canal basin was built with the wharves and warehouses for coal, agricultural machinery, stone, bricks, and timber etc., In fact all the heavy bulk commodities that were never a commercial proposition until bulk movement across the length and breadth of the country became possible.

The prime commodity—coal, came from the Derbyshire coalfield, mainly Shipley Colliery. As a result the coal wharf was called Shipley Wharf and when the canal ceased to be and it became a railway coal yard it retained the title—Old Shipley Wharf. This is a an interesting example of the caprice of history where a name from a district far away can be imported and the term wharf be retained for a location that is plainly not a wharf in later years, a recollection of things past!

After the Liverpool & Manchester Railway celebrations in 1830 the world was left in little doubt which way modern transport was heading. The mighty undertaking of the building of the London & Birmingham Railway under the responsibility of one Robert Stephenson is now part of the historical tableux of mid-nineteenth century England. The opening of the main line in 1838 together with the opening of the Grand Junction Railway from Birmingham to the north-west in 1837 meant that the engineering workshop of the world -Birmingham, was linked with the 'Cottonopolis' of Manchester and its satellite towns together with the major port of Liverpool.

Once again Newport Pagnell was so near to this main stream and yet so far, a mere four miles. Although coaches and wagons did begin meeting trains at Denbigh Hall on the main line.

It appears that the canal was not the unqualified success that the promoters had hoped. Whilst the town was affected in a deleterious way by opening of the main line. Within six years all of the busy through road traffic had been reduced to a mere thirty vehicles a week, the town must have seemed comparatively empty and depressed.

In 1845 matters were put in hand that were likely to change all of that. A successful Bill for a railway from Bletchley to Bedford was under construction in that year. Consequently a company was formed to join it, with a junction at Wolverton with the main line, then east to Newport Pagnell, continuing south through Moulsoe, Broughton, Salford joining the new railway at a junction where the present Ridgmont station is situated.

6

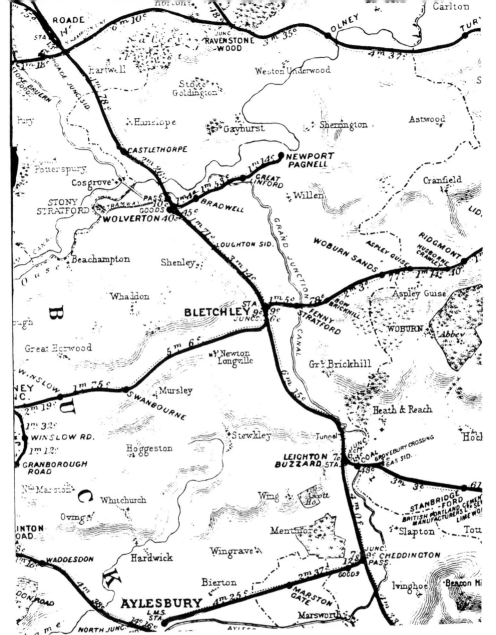

The area of Newport Pagnell between Bletchley, and Roade. The line of the 1846 survey was from Wolverton to Ridgmont, the station on the Bletchley — Bedford line. The later proposal of the line when built was that it should be extended to Olney and later Wellinborough. The unfulfilled hopes of this plan are related in the text, this is how the layout of the lines remained.

Bill Simpson Collection

7

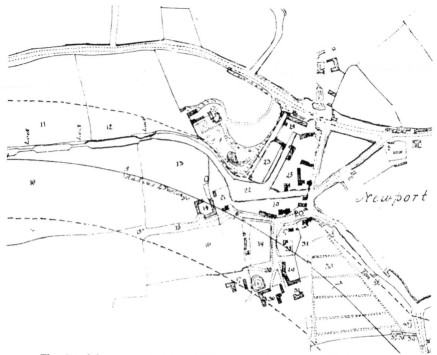

The site of the proposed station at Newport on the survey of the Wolverton, Newport Pagnell and Bedford Railway (1846). The main interest of this unsuccessful scheme is that it shows the canal basin and wharf buildings. The Newport Pagnell Canal was 2,100 yards long.

Geoffrey Webb Collection

The company was named Wolverton, Newport Pagnell & Bedford Railway and a meeting was held to form it at the Swan Hotel, Newport Pagnell in June 1844. The stated distance of the line was 15½ miles.

On the 6 January, 1846 a notice was delivered to the clerk of the Newport Pagnell Canal Co. that an application would be made in the next session of parliament for an Act to construct a line from Wolverton to Newport Pagnell then continue to join the Bedford Line. The note stated that part of the land of the canal and certain building will be required and is sounding out the feeling of the proprietors. Their reaction was to offer the entire canal for sale to the railway. In February the railway promoters offered £10,000 which was unhesitatingly accepted.

At that time the station at Wolverton was the second station, south of

SHIPLEY WHARF.

NEWPORT PAGNEL, 1840
Mr. *Foster* *April 10*
Bought of WILLIAM SAUNDERSON

	tons.	cwts.	qrs.	bus.	price	£	s.	d.
Old Shipley, durable hard								
Shipley, blazing hard								
Ditto, bright cementing								
Slack, for lime and brick burning								
Moira Coal								
Wednesbury Ditto								
Common Coal								
Cokes		15				189		
Oil Cake								
Salt								
Lime								
Cement								
Slate								
Brick								
Tiles								
Timber								
Deals								
Lath								
Grindstones								
Carriage								
						£		

Two-pence per Cwt. will be taken off if paid for within six weeks of delivery.

An invoice to Mr Foster from William Saunderson for 15 cwt of coke on Shipley Wharf of the Newport Pagnell Canal Co in 1840.

John Coales Collection

Public Wharf, Newport Pagnel.

Mr. *Troutsmith* 1844
Bought of AARON LAW.

Cwt.		£	s.	d.
20 *Best*	Coals at /4 per Cwt.	3	4	
3	Coke		1	3
	Discount for Money 2d Cwt.			

The wharf at Newport Pagnell before the railway when coal was bought from Aaron Law in 1844 supplied from the Canal.

John Coales Collection

9

London and North Western Railway Company.

Wolverton

Receive from HIVES AND SON.

Cwt.	Qrs.	Bus.	*(to own Team)*
7	6		*Wheat to the order of*
			Edmund Lythall Esq
	16	*Sacks*	*Radford Hall*
			near Leamington
Carriage paid			*Sum 6/11¾*

Waybill for Hives & Son that had the siding at the back of the station to their mill. Sixteen sacks of wheat to Radford Hall near Leamington on the LNWR in 1865. Note that it had to be carted to Wolverton station at this time. Four years later with the opening of the branch during 1869, 15,643 tons of general goods were conveyed from and to the town and 23,366 tons of coal came up the branch. Passenger receipts were £1,854. From January the monthly increase achieved double the tonnage by December.

John Coales Collection

the Stratford Road and not the original one built by the L & B that was subsequently absorbed by the entire works milieu. The levels were entirely different on this survey than the subsequent line. At 2 miles 3 chains the line was to pass *under* the Grand Junction Canal, rather than the line as built, which passed over it.

The line proposed was not popular with the Bedford Railway, indeed there appears little gain in it for them being foisted with an unnecessary junction. Whilst the Duke of Bedford openly castigated the plan.

Once in the parliamentary chambers criticism was upheld that the purchasing powers for the Newport Pagnell Canal had not been sufficiently advertised which caused the Bill to be withdrawn. To what extent this was effected by its adversaries will never be known, but Newport Pagnell had lost out for the first railway opportunity.

Another interesting scheme that was being drawn up at the same time was a Bletchley, Newport Pagnell, Olney, Wellingborough line. Originally proposed in the L & B period of 1845 it was continued by the LNWR which absorbed the L & B, Grand Junction, Manchester & Birmingham Railways in June 1846 This scheme was another foray in the territorial wars that railway companies thrust and parried throughout the 1840's and 50's. The plan was to shorten the distance to Peterborough before the Great Northern Railway built their own line empowered by an Act of 1846. This scheme would have produced an entirely different look to the site of the railway station at Newport Pagnell as the line passed through the town on a south to north axis rather than west to east, still crossing the area known as 'The Green'.

However, this plan fared no better than the other as the LNWR appeared to have second thoughts in the light of the GNR's apparent success in reaching Peterborough and withdrew the plan, even though the Act had been achieved in 1847.

Another scheme promoted by the LNWR was the Bletchley, Newport Pagnell, Northampton line of 1859 aimed at improving the service for Northampton which had been poorly served at the end of a branch from Blisworth although this was extended to Peterborough in 1845. The incorporation of a Bedford & Northampton Railway with Midland Railway affiliations had no little bearing on this. A town worth retention looked like being taken by a rival company. The LNWR scheme did not go ahead however, probably out of boardroom reasoning and argument that a greater scheme in the future of the LNWR would suit their needs better. What this transpired to be was the quadrupling plans of 1875 and a junction at Roade for the Northampton line. Once again Newport Pagnell had been cut out of the reckoning, still without direct railway communication.

Finally, on 29 June 1863 the Newport Pagnell Railway Company were authorised by parliament to build their line. This also did not see the town as a terminus as powers were obtained on the 2 June 1865 to extend the line a further 5½ miles to Olney. (Capital £80,000). Further, on the 10 August 1866 powers were obtained to extend the line to join the Northampton - Peterborough line of the LNWR. The tricky part is the desire to form a junction at Olney with the Midland Railway who controlled the aforementioned line from Bedford & Northampton. This certainly was likely to incur some furrowed brows in the boardroom of the LNWR, as it courted the interests of rivals at each end of a short line.

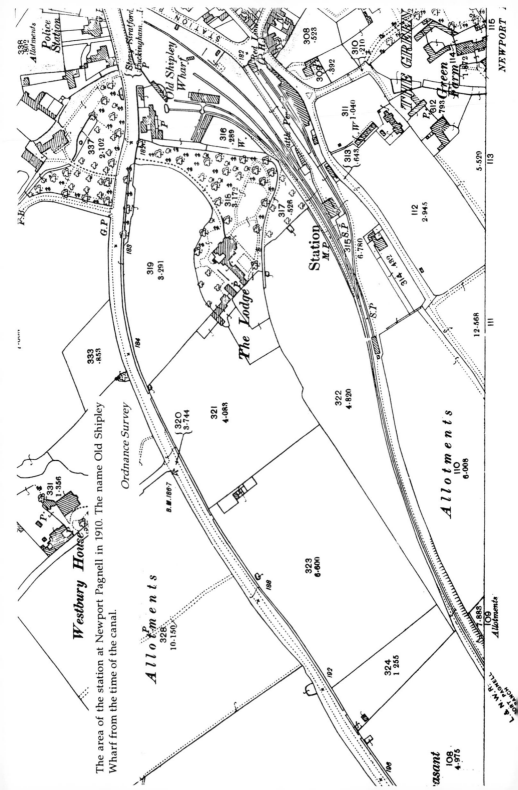

The area of the station at Newport Pagnell in 1910. The name Old Shipley Wharf from the time of the canal.

Ordnance Survey

The connection at Olney had been laid out as 'up' and 'down' burrowing junction. Ambitious beyond a branch line usage. A later Act of 1871 abandoned this type of connection simply running into Olney station.

In 1858 the station at Wolverton was rebuilt south of the Stratford Road on the area now occupied by Paint Shops. Removing it for the first time out of the confines of the works. This altered the survey from the one originally carried out for the branch by Robert Stephenson in 1845. The railway now ran over the canal at Black Horse Bridge not beneath it. Gradients were none the less quite taxing.

Newport Pagnell Railway Co.

As if to emphasize the desperate need for connecting transport in the area a Mr G Paternoster began one of the earliest omnibus services connecting up with various railheads in the district. This was for the conveyance of passengers and parcels from the Ram Inn, Newport Pagnell for Dunstable and Luton every Tuesday and Friday mornings at 10 o'clock. Return from the Crown Inn, Luton for Dunstable, Woburn Sands and Newport Pagnell every Wednesday and Saturday mornings at 11.30. There was also a service between Wolverton, Newport and Olney three times daily and Wolverton and Stony Stratford. This was in 1860.

In the same year the Board of Trade reported on the objectives of the Railway Company. To incorporate capital of £45,000 in shares and £15,000 in loans. For a line to be 3 miles 69 chains. The Act to include powers to purchase the Newport Pagnell Canal Co., (a retained clause from the 1845 Bill), and to make a working agreement with the LNWR. This latter dependency with the larger company proved to be a thornier association than foreseen. Any disharmony seems all the more regrettable in view of the close interests of both companies. In September 1861 the pressure of need for housing for works employees was relieved by an overspill development at Stantonbury (Bradwell) where workers houses became newly tenanted after their construction by the LNWR. Of the 2,000 work employees half lived at Stantonbury. Moreover, the company planned to have another two-hundred houses occupied by September of the following year at Wolverton. Development was taking on pace before the railway was opened and would continue to the end of the century.

The need for a railway passing through the locality is clearly expressed by the managers of the following concerns.

13

Newport Pagnell railway station early this century showing it purely as an LNWR station. The suitably imposing station sign on the right with cast letters painted white on a dark blue or black background. Years later a pathetic piece of planking replaced it in very marked contrast. Seen to the left the cattle pen and landing was built in 1877 shortly after the line was taken over by the LNWR.

Mrs J Graham

Joseph Palmer, a tanner at Olney uses 100 tons of coal a year. He is secretary of the gasworks which uses 300 tons of coal from Birchwood Colliery which now comes from Sharnbrook on the Midland Railway. He has purchased £100 in shares. The Secretary of the gas company at Newport Pagnell was Mr Richard Shepherd an architect and surveyor. The price of gas coal is 20 shillings a ton delivered to the works. He expects the cost to be reduced to 4 shillings (20p) a ton by rail. This coal also comes from Birchwood Colliery across Midland Railway metals.

Mr Odell, Ironmonger and general dealer at Newport Pagnell sends 300 tons of goods each year to London at a cost of 5 shillings (25p) per ton. Charles Mason, general goods manager of the LNWR states that goods are carted between Wolverton and Newport Pagnell by an agent at the following rates:

First Class and Second Class 4 shillings 10 pence (24p) per ton,
   3 pence (1p) per cwt.
Third Class 6 shillings 6 pence (32½p) per ton.
Fourth Class 9 shillings 6 pence (47½p) per ton.
Fifth Class 12 shillings 6 pence (62½p) per ton.

The charge by rail would simply be 3 shillings (15p) between railheads.

On a personal level the sympathy of the LNWR locally was without question in this evidence for promotion of the line by Mr J.E. McConnell Locomotive Superintendent of the LNWR and resident for some 15 years from 1847 at Wolverton Locomotive Works.

'About half the workmen have to travel a considerable distance, as much as four or five miles including Newport Pagnell. It must be a great strain on the men – it is equal to ten per cent of their labour. In winter when the roads were heavy the poor fellows were nearly done in'. Shortly after the passing of the Act the directors of the NPR were not slow in taking up the point made by McConnell to the boardroom at Euston. Stating further that Newport Pagnell contains two breweries, steam and water flour mills, gas works, coach manufactory, the original works of Aston Martin and that very considerable traffic is carried by road or canal to the Sharnbrook Station of the Midland Railway. A point made in commercial innocence by the NPR that probably played on the sensitivity of some LNWR, directors. The Midland at that time was seen as an upstart by the LNWR. This memorial, intended to bring greater support from the LNWR was delivered by the board of the new company namely:

John Dollin Basset, Joseph Palmer, William Bateman Bull, George Gooch, Thomas Taylor and Richard Sheppard in November 1863.

The purchase price of the canal was £9,000 a drop of a £1,000 from the 1845 Bill. The Grand Junction Canal tried to suppress the railway in parliament but failed to do so. The canal branch had not been one of the more lucrative investments of the age. Its maximum dividend of 6% occurred in 1845, some years were 3% most were nil! The canal was closed by the NPR in September 1864 which was practically necessary but would represent some three years without return on the capital outlay of the purchase price.

News of the line's success was greeted with jubilation in Newport Pagnell ringing out the church bells in celebration. One could imagine that nowadays the announcement of a new motorway or by-pass would receive little more than resignation and relief.

The Survey of the line began at that time from a junction in the Wolverton Station sited in 1858 and not the present one. It began with a curve of two-furlong radius. Most of the line was either on embankment or in a cutting with 138,674 yards of the former and 193,000 yards of the latter. The lattice girder bridge over the Grand Junction Canal at Linford to be 30 ft wide with 9 ft of headroom. It was built of wrought iron at Lennard Brothers in Wales, the span is eighty-two feet. It was sent in sections and rivetted together on the side of the canal after which it was rolled across between the two abutments. To effect this two canal boats were fastened together and timber framing erected upon them to carry the end of each girder across. Cross girders were then fitted between the beams at about five feet apart and upon these planking was bolted down to take the ballast and the rails. Headway over the canal is ten feet. Linford Station is under construction at the same time as the building of the line. After Linford cutting the line follows the former route of the canal.

Contractors for the line Messrs Bray and Wilson. Directors remuneration was fixed at £200 pa and the salary of the Secretary £300 pa.

No clear indication when the first sod was cut but works are in progress in August 1864. Half the capital had been paid up and therefore the company was in a position to exercise their borrowing powers up to £15,000.

Rather oddly work proceeded with some enthusiasm until May 1865 when everything was stopped and the labourers were paid off without explanation.

The hiatus appears to have lasted little more than a week before restarting with redoubled enthusiasm. It was expected that the entire line would be complete and ready for traffic by August 1865. As the Bill for the

The station at Newport Pagnell looking east. A good clear study of the ground frame on the right put in with the take over of the line by the LNWR, opposite is an LNWR ground signal. To use the run-round loop at Newport Pagnell it was necessary to run beyond the platform 'STOP' signal into the goods yard.

A Swain

extension was passing through parliament at the same time and was expecting to become an Act in the very near future it was hoped that the line could be proceeded with immediately. The only feature that brought particular censure from the Board of Trade was that the railway should cross the turnpike road at Newport Pagnell on a bridge without risk to townspeople.

This was agreed, after some deliberation as the company would have, not surprisingly, preferred a level crossing. A statement at a meeting at the Swan Hotel on the 30 June 1865 by the chairman remarked that level crossings were undesirable but 'in this case it would only be a single line and there could not be a great number of trains daily. This must have been a bit tongue-in-cheek when the railway was hoping to connect with Wellingborough and the east Midlands. Gleaning all the advantages of that connection would certainly require more than five trains per day and with equal certainty another set of rails. The upshot was that the Board of

The railway bridge that never had a train. This bridge spanned the Wolverton Road at Newport Pagnell and was built to take the Olney extension. The fact that such a major structure on the project had been completed shows how very near this section of line came to realizing completion. It was built in 1866 and was demolished sometime in the 1870's. The LNWR charged the defunct Newport Pagnell Railway Company for demolition but did in fact fill in the arches with timber to use them for storage, clearly evident in the photograph.

Wolverton & District Archeological Society.

Trade held them to law and the bridge was built — but not the railway extension that was planned to pass over it.

On the NPR the first train ran from Wolverton on Saturday 30 September 1865. It was a train of 17 ballast wagons filled with navvies. This artisan express raised a welcoming cheer on its arrival at Newport Pagnell and by reputation probably several hundred more within the

A constant problem for Newport Pagnell are the transgressions of the River Lovat on the lower reaches at Tickford. Flooding occurred as recently as the wet period of 1992. This view believed to be the floods in April 1908 shows workmen having arrived home from the carriage works at Wolverton being transported through the waters by carts. This being the entrance to the station it is faintly visible in the background on the original print. Also faintly visible on the extreme right is the Webb 2-4-2 tank that has brought their train in with what could possibly be four-wheel stock. The building on the left is Coales weighbridge office.

Bill West Collection.

nearby inn called 'The Flowing Tankard'. The sight of a train reaching Newport Pagnell must have caused relief to one George Labrum who had started his business at the 'Wrestlers Inn' in the March of that year in anticipation of the railway opening.

The close juxposition in time of the line's completion and the Olney extension being started is clearly expressed as the work began two weeks

Newport Pagnell on the 10 of April 1948 two footplatemen in the foreground and Guard on left Ron Webb, driver George Padmore and on the engine W Dryden. The former LNWR Coal Tank 27561 is about to depart with the 1.12 pm to Wolverton. Before this departure the engine would have shunted the goods vehicles on the adjoining siding. On reaching Wolverton he will hand over the staff for the line to the duty goods train that will then enter the branch and bring and collect the goods from here and Bradwell.

H C Casserley

Same train seen from a different angle. Engine 27561 survived to become British Railways 58881 but was finally withdrawn in September 1950.

H C Casserley

The locomotive shed at Newport Pagnell and small coaling platform in April 1948. The signal arm at the top of the post was a 'fixed home' trains arrived by the small 'calling on' arm beneath it. To this day the signal post remains to mark this spot as British Rail donated it, but it was never collected, by a local school.

H C Casserley

later on the 12 October. All the stone, bricks, lime, sleepers and iron rails had been placed in position.

It appeared that although the line was to every intent and purpose complete, proper arrangements had not been made at Wolverton with the junction connection with the LNWR who were asking £500 pa. from the company for the use of Wolverton station.

Another factor was that the contractor was to supply staff and rolling stock to work the line for a fixed percentage of the gross receipts. Further at the 1 May 1866 a government inspector had not visited the line.

On 8 May 1866 Captain Rich R E Government Inspector visited the line and pronounced it to be in working order, with the exception of some slight alterations necessary at Wolverton.

First notice of suspension of work on the Olney extension was on the 2 June 1866. Construction had been taking place for some eight months or so.

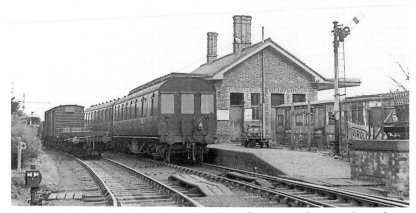

Newport Pagnell on the 10 April 1948 with a train about to leave for Wolverton. The coach body on the right is believed to be an ex- North London Railway Third No. 1101 deposited in August 1921 The few goods wagons are waiting for collection. A special daily working.

H C Casserley.

NEWPORT PAGNELL

SPARE: 1. 10. 12.

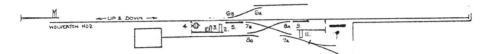

Signalling diagram for Newport Pagnell. It was often the practice at the station to run against the 'up' platform starter signal' leaving the 'down' calling-on arm in the clear position. The point setting is identical and with only one engine on the branch seems safe. However, the exception proves the rule through casual familiarity. A loco went to coal at the stage in 1926 then reversed back onto its train. Upon leaving for Wolverton it continued down the shed road, through the doors, the back of the shed and into a ditch! With the introduction of 'Lock & Block' and the removal of request stop signals at the two intermediate stations the line signalling for the last sixty years was as follows.

Newport Pagnell	'down'	Fixed distant
		Fixed Home
		Calling-on Signal
		Ground signal for movements from sidings and loop to single line.
		Circular semaphore on platform stencilled 'Stop Await Instructions' to enter yard.
	'up'	platform starter
Wolverton	'down'	Platform starter
	'up'	Fixed distant
		Station home

The lever signal frame at Newport Pagnell of 1884. From left to right the levers are identified thus: 1 - spare; 2 - space; 3 - Down line calling-on signal; 4 - ground signal from main to goods shed siding behind the station, originally Hives; 5 - locks points 7 and 8; 6 - main and trap goods shed siding; 7 - main and trap siding; 8 - Spare, but once, main and trap engine shed siding; 9 - 8 points locked and unlocked. 10 - space; 11 - space; 12 - platform starting signal. The 'down' home signal is fixed, the calling-on arm beneath it is no 3 signal. Signal no 4 stands at the foot of this post. The points 7 are at the Wolverton end of the run-round loop. This is linked to an LNWR rotating ground signal. The other end of this loop is controlled by a ground frame released by Annett's key which is held in the station office.

Ray Bailey

The workmen's train having arrived at Newport runs round the coaches to push them down the yard.

K C H Fairey.

In order to get some traffic under way, that is to say goods, the NPR arranged with the LNWR to use Wolverton station at a third of £500 pa; and for working the junction by day only £80 pa. Thereby the line tentatively opened on 24 July 1866. Financial constraints, difficulties with arrangements with the contractor and with the Government Inspector concerning the junction had compounded into delay for the passenger traffic. It had been earnestly hoped by the Board that before their half-yearly meeting on 7 August 1866 that all would have been underway.

By 18 January 1867 the proper connection had not been put in between the LNWR and NPR at Wolverton. The LNWR Special Committee minuted on that date that they would contact the Clearing House Secretary as to the money due from the Newport Pagnell Railway Co. for through goods booking with them that had not been paid for and should be stopped.

At a further meeting 12 April 1867 the Manager reported that £440. on account of the cost of putting in their junction at Wolverton had been paid to the LNWR and therefore Mr Woodhouse the LNWR Agent was authorised to put in the junction and signals at a cost of £567. This was begun at the end of the month.

The 'Nobby Goods' ageing Webb Coal Tank gets to grips with the daily goods at Newport Pagnell

Arthur Grigg

In view of probable opening of the NPR a public meeting was held at the Swan Hotel 5 July 1867 with a view to establishing a corn and cattle market. A proposal that received the warmest support from J. Talbot, Traffic Manager of NPR who rightly proclaimed the support of the new railway that will be ready to receive *all* traffic in a few weeks time.

In the spirit of optimism the new market opened and trucks were made available at the station for cattle and sheep whilst dealers were allowed to travel free until the line was open for regular passenger traffic.

However, an editorial in the Newport Pagnell Gazetter on the 3 August 1867 severely criticizes the NPR for delay and a year of several bogus dates being announced only proving eventually to have falsely raised expectations. The Directors must have been wondering uneasily which one of them would eventually face the pilloried wrath of the townspeople. Especially those working at the locomotive works that had just endured another winter which they were probably hoping to have avoided trudging through.

Finally Colonel Rich the Government Inspector came and viewed the final works of connection and appeared to be satisfied.

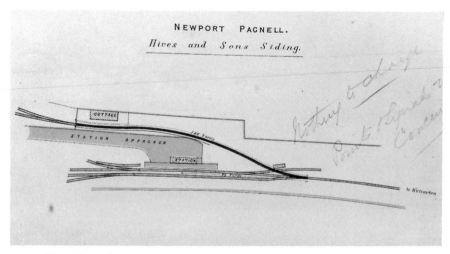

NEWPORT PAGNELL.

Hives and Sons Siding.

The siding that ran past the front of the station to Hives Flour Mill. The Mill later became the business of Coales & Son. Thereby a building that had seen use by canal and railway survived until after closure of the branch using road transport.

John Pritchett Collection

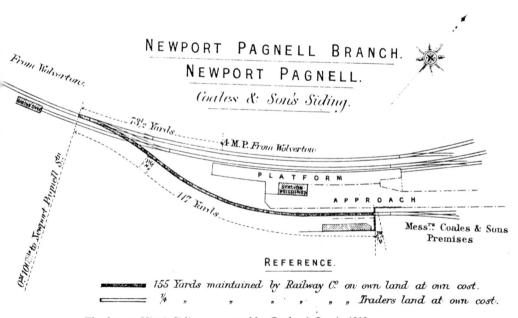

NEWPORT PAGNELL BRANCH.

NEWPORT PAGNELL.

Coales & Sons Siding.

REFERENCE.

155 Yards maintained by Railway C? on own land at own cost.
¼ „ „ „ „ „ „ „ Traders land at own cost.

The former Hive's Siding now used by Coales & Son in 1910.

John Pritchett Collection

26

The siding alongside Hives, later Coales Mill. Presumably the wagons brimming with coal have recently been shunted over from the station.

John Coales Collection

The entrance to Coales Mill alongside the station entrance. Between them the weighbridge and office.

John Coales Collection

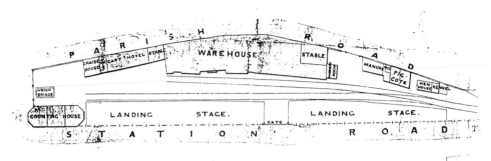

Ground plan of Coales Mill enclosing the sidings.

John Coales Collection

On Monday 2 September 1867 the line was opened completely as the local press announced sarcastically 'Notwithstanding the general incredulity respecting the opening of the railway the trains did run and the timetable issued that day.'

Bearing away their earlier frustrations the town gathered itself to a just cause for celebration. Under fair weather skies the Wolverton Brass Band and the Drum and Fife Band met the first train from Newport Pagnell with mellifluous accompaniment as it left Newport shortly after 1 o'clock with every carriage overflowing. A large concourse of officials and workmen cheered the occupants. On its return the train carried with it the bandsmen who must have travelled on the train, who on arrival at the town marched through the streets to the heavily decorated Swan Hotel. The day continued with 'rustic sports' with flat racing from men and boys, donkey race, also with riders sitting backwards, greasy pole climb, scrambling for caps, handkerchiefs, mufflers, toys. Whilst above it all the timbre of church bells gave notice of their approval. The station was ornamented with flags and the entrance to the town from Wolverton by road was decorated with evergreens. In the evening there was illuminations of a large star and Prince of Wales's Feathers and strands of Chinese lanterns.

Certainly the townspeople were making up for disappointments as the celebrations continued until the early hours of the following morning.

On the following day the festivities were still unabated as tea and tobacco were given to all persons over 60 years of age (the report does not say by whom). Sports continued and enthusiastic announcements were

28

Situated on a distant curve the goods shed at Newport Pagnell is little evident on views of the station, it is therefore fortunate that this view was taken including it. The rails ran alongside the canopy overhang.

A Swain.

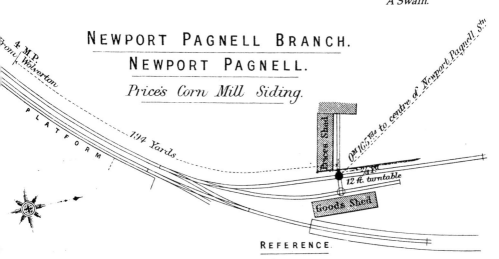

NEWPORT PAGNELL BRANCH.
NEWPORT PAGNELL.
Prices Corn Mill Siding.

from Wolverton • 4 M.P.

PLATFORM

194 Yards

Price's Shed

0ᵐ 165 Yds. to centre of Newport Pagnell Stⁿ

12 ft. turntable

Goods Shed

REFERENCE.

²/₃ Yards maintained by Traders on Railway Cᵒˢ land at own cost.
12 Fᵗ Turntable colored Red „ „ Railway Cᵒ on own land at own cost.

Siding for George Price, Corn, Cake, Coal, Lime merchant and brick maker. A siding installed in 1871 labouriously at right angles via a 12ft turntable worked by man and horse. Shunting horses were still being used at the station in the early fifties. Notice the rails of the other siding enclosed in a curved rectangle. This is almost certainly the truncated Olney extension leading onto the viaduct.

John Pritchett Collection

29

Newport Pagnell High Street in the early twenties. The England of small towns with that happy mix of architectural style. All retained on a human scale with roads pleasurably easy to cross. Population in 1801: 2,048 by 1901 this had reached: 4,028

Ray Bailey

made about a further 500 to 600 houses being needed to accommodate people coming to work at Wolverton Works. Also the installation of the electric telegraph.

The new timetable advertised six trains in each direction daily with two each way on Sundays. By December it was eight passenger trains each way and two goods.

Judging by reports the only station between the junction and the terminus was Linford.

On the subject of horse omnibuses a local user describes them as a 'black box on four wheels more like a death-shaking machine used in the inquisition. The horse used was twenty-five years old and passengers had to walk up the hills. On a wet day it was usually impossible to find space inside the vehicle and was therefore necessary to sit outside.'

Throughout 1868 complaints ranged from unlit Third Class coaches,

The local train waits patiently for custom at Newport Pagnell station in July 1964. Note the height of the horse and cattle dock built as an extension to the main original platform in 1877.

K C H Fairey

noisy trains on Saturday night and during the worst months of January and February the quagmire on the approach to the station, which suggests that no surfaced and drained road as yet existed.

Special race trains ran in March to Newport Pagnell Races.

There were serious arguments with the LNWR on rental costs when the NPR denied agreeing to the cost of £500 per annum for the use of Wolverton station. The LNWR then threatened to stop money owing to the NPR for through bookings of passengers and goods.

An aside to events was the effect of large scale reorganisation at Wolverton Works. On the 22 January 1870 it was noted that 26 locos had left Wolverton for Crewe with a further 40 due shortly. This was the beginning of centralising loco work at Crewe and carriage work at Wolverton. The effect of this is familiar enough in present times, many families would have to face upheaval to follow their employment.

On 21 January 1870 the LNWR Special Committee agree to lend an engine to the NPR on daily repayment for its use.

A good view of the shed at Newport Pagnell showing the construction of corrugated iron. Ivatt 41222 is appropriately installed alongside the coaling platform. This scene in the early 1950's.

R Butterfield.

The impression given by the LNWR at this time seems surprisingly obstructive and disinclined to budge an inch to make things easier for the NPR.

LNWR Special Committee 3 March 1870 Notice of Special Meeting with a view to expelling the NPR from the Clearing Association. Mr Cawkwell reported that he is in negotiation with the parties involved with a view to undertaking the working of the line charging the NPR £1250 a year rent for services at Wolverton for engines and carriages, maintenance of the permanent way and for staff at Newport Pagnell.

Throughout 1870 the NPR and LNWR are at loggerheads the former believing it was paying its dues as the latter was keeping all the monies taken at Wolverton.

Hostility by the LNWR spread to the Olney extension matter which they obstructed as the Midland was favourably inclined to a connection at

'Newport Nobby' approaching the station with the 8.33 from Wolverton on an August morning in 1964.

Peter Baughan.

Olney. The NPR felt that they were unfairly treated by the LNWR as the little line brought goods tonnage of £1,000 per year of about 12,000 tons while the passenger traffic receipts were £1854 2s 7d (£1854.13p) (for 1869) yet the small company had still to pay £500 per year to the LNWR. One Director said that it was like a shopkeeper charging his customers to come into his shop.

The NPR were very keen on the Olney extension to break the LNWR monopoly, if they became connected with the Bedford to Northampton

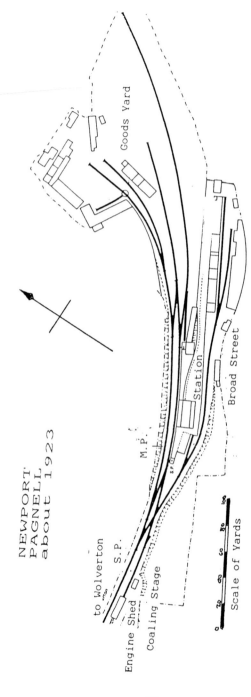

NEWPORT
PAGNELL
about 1923

to Wolverton

S.P.

Engine Shed

Coaling Stage

M.P.

S.P.

Station

Broad Street

Goods Yard

Scale of Yards

Newport Pagnell station at the time of the grouping.

Fred Bateman Collection

34

line, the Board believed the cartage of coal would be cheaper via Wellingborough from the Leicestershire and Derbyshire coalfields rather than via Rugby on the LNWR. A possibility not likely to have escaped the notice of the LNWR and a great deal to do with the rancour. On the meeting of 8 March 1870 one of the Directors Mr Bull made the proposal 'That in the opinion of this meeting, a continuation and completion of the Newport Pagnell Railway, and its junction with the Northampton & Bedford line now in construction, will afford great facility for passenger and goods traffic to and from this town and neighbourhood and give a more speedily access to all parts of the United Kingdom'. This proposal was carried unanimously.

The reality of the situation eventually transpired in June 1870 when it was found that the NPR could not meet the debts and liabilities incurred by the rights of the Acts of 1863 and 1865 amounting to £41,000.

As a result a Bill was filed in the Court of Chancery by William Robert Galbraith on behalf of himself and other creditors of the company and a receiver of the tolls and profits was appointed.

Almost compounding the financial problems Stewart S Talbot Manager of the Company became bankrupt.

Throughout 1870-71 the line and its proposed extension was in financial hot water with outstanding debts on existing work and material done for the extension but without being remotely in sight of having it in revenue earning service.

Whilst the working part of the connection was not, thanks to little support from the LNWR, receiving enough monies to cover its liabilities outstanding.

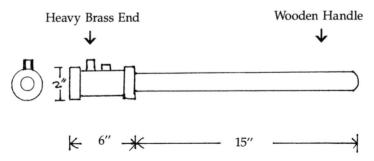

The Staff used on the Newport Pagnell branch, drawn by former driver and Area Supervisor Fred Bateman. It was coloured red and held in the foreman's office at Wolverton and the booking office at Newport Pagnell
Fred Bateman

Obviously the only assuaging course was to have the line purchased by the LNWR.

It appears that the frustrations of the Olney connection and the exacting tolls introduced by the LNWR were having a deleterious affect on the little company. The LNWR Special Committee minuted in July that the NPR were interested in the LNWR working the line entirely upon securing a net profit for the shareholders of the NPR. This was referred to Mr Cawkwell, Chairman.

The following month in desperate circumstances the NPR are pressuring the LNWR to reduce their charges at Wolverton to more liberal costs.

Although 1873 seems to have been a very uncertain time for the NPR at least they were able to bring 3,000 persons to the town on Monday 13 April of Newport Pagnell Steeplechases.

Finally, on 3 July 1873 the LNWR received the communication which they must have been, to put it mildly, anticipating. That the NPR wished to sell their railway to the LNWR and were prepared to enter negotiations on price. They were at that time, as claimed by the LNWR, to be in their debt to £1727.

The LNWR's reply to this was that subject to the abandonment of the Olney extension they would be willing to take the line in perpetuity at a net rental of £2,000 per annum or purchase for a capital sum of £50,000, 16 January 1874.

The result was that the NPR were prepared to accept the offer of annual rental whilst rowers were sought from parliament to make a direct sale, which would probably take two years.

A special meeting was called on 20 May 1875 at the Westminster Chambers of a Mr J. Borradaile where it was agreed to abandon the much vaunted extension to Olney, this must have been a very bitter pill to

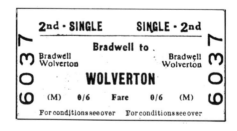

36

swallow. The line was absorbed by the LNWR on 29 June 1875. Powers for the line beyond Olney had been abandoned on 25 May 1871.

Prior to completion of purchase the LNWR survey of the ways and works on the line throws some interesting light on its condition and appearance.

25 June 1875

Signal:-

> There are 'home' and 'distant' signals at each station but the 'distant' signals are not worked and are out of repair. The 'home' signals at *Bradwell* and *Linford* are worked for the purpose of stopping trains when there are passengers to pick up.

At the beginning of the branch operations there were two signalmen employed at Wolverton paid £1. per week. A signal box existed on the curve before the junction.

Level Crossings:-

> There are none for the public highway and therefore no gatemen are required.

Train Staff & Tickets:-

> None in operation as there is only one engine in steam on the line. One train per day is 'parliamentary',* this is run in the early morning calling at Linford for the Wolverton workmen. Weekly tickets for works trains are issued 1s 6d (7½p) for men 1s 0d (5p) for boys.

Details of Wylie's Siding at Bradwell.

> It was laid by the company on Mr Wylie's land for the right of which the company pay £6. per annum. The lease is for 21 years and is dated from 10 August 1870. It is also shared by coal dealers who must pay 1s 0d (5p) per truck for wharfage. Traffic is worked to the siding by a daily trip from Wolverton. The siding averaged 5 to 10 trucks per week delivered 40 tons of coal and about 30 tons of lime. The siding points are padlocked.

---

* Regulation of Railways Act 1844. By this Act all railways in the country were compelled to run at least one train each day serving every station. This to include closed carriages for third class passengers at a fare of 1 penny per mile 'Parliamentaries'.

Details on Sidings at Newport Pagnell:-

Hives & Son Siding. This is laid partly on their own property and partly on NPR Company property. No rent is paid by Hives & Son for the siding.

Price's Siding on Company's land. No rent is paid by Price. He has a siding of his own at right angles to the one belonging to the Company. The extension line on a viaduct over the goods yard is partly on NPR Company's ground.

Bradwell Station.

Bradwell had adjoining an eight room cottage, belonging to the NPR but there was none at Linford.

Waiting Room - 3 chairs, blind, Looking glass. Booking Office — 3 chairs, Office lamp. Fire grate, fender. fire irons, Clock (double faced), Ticket case (75 tubes), dating press & types, Counter fitted with drawers, ruler etc., Coal cellar, 1 oil lamp, 1 dist. Signal lamp, 1 oil can, 3 oil sockets for station lamps, 1 Broom, Platform — 3 lamps, 1 Byelaws in frame, 1 Name Board, 2 Distant signals & levers (not in use) — 1 Home Signal (in use), 1 Siding Indicator (not in order) 1 pump (No water).

Linford Station:

Waiting Room - 3 Chairs.

Booking Office - 6 Chairs, Looking glass, Firegrate, fender, fire irons (broken) Clock (two faces), Dating Press, Ticket box (75 tubes), ruler, Counter with drawers.

Coal Cellar - Small Notice Board, 3 Signal lamps for Distant & Home signals.

Platform - 2 Lamps, 1 Lime Bill Board, 1 Byelaws in frame, 2 levers for Distant Signals (not in use), 1 Home signal, 2 cisterns for platform oil lamps, Pump (no water), 2 Hand lamps, 1 Oil can, 1 Oil feeder, 1 Name Board.

Both stations have WC & Urinal (1 stall) but the walls are in a very damp condition from the tanks being leaky. The waiting room at Linford is also in a very bad condition from water leakage. The name boards at each place require repainting.

Return of the great tenor bell to Newport Church after re-casting on the 12 June 1911. The yard crane has obviously played an essential role in proceedings whilst the driver and fireman of the Webb 2-4-2 tank look on, in the background. In our present automated age it is little realised that horses served a widespread haulage need as recently as the 1950's when they were still used for shunting wagons in Newport goods yard. Should it not be clear on printing the lettering on the coal wagon behind the crane is 'LNWR' and the number on the end '51649'.

Bill West Collection.

Goods Traffic:-

 Average total of mileage & terminals paid monthly to the Newport Pagnell Co. = £95.

 Allowance on goods at full c&d rates 4s 0d (20p) per ton terminals.

 Special Class 1s 6d (7½p) per ton to terminals.

 and 1d per ton per mile or 4d (2p) mileage.

 Minerals (Stone etc) 9d (3½p) terminals.

      2d (1p) mileage.

 Coals (formerly 1s 0d (5p) 10½d (4p) per ton.

 Cattle   1s 0d (5p) per truck.

The Bradwell traffic, at which place only full loads are accommodated averages from 5 to 10 trucks of station to station traffic, 40 tons of coal and about 30 tons of Lime. Goods trains are worked thus; Goods for Newport leave Wolverton by the first passenger train at 6.30am whilst outward goods leave Newport at 6.05pm.

Carting is done at Newport by horse & cart belonging to the NPR.

Effectively the Newport Pagnell Railway was dissolved by an Act of 29 June 1875, The LNWR paid to the Shareholders of the Company the sum of £50,000 less £2,724 16s 4d (£2724.82p) owing to them. Also deductible from this payment, as if to rub salt into the wounds. Costs of the Act; Payment of Land Charges; Removing Bridges (this being the Olney extension bridge at Newport Pagnell); Paying Mortgage Debts of the Company; Costs of winding up the Company.

Details of workmens trains running on the branch: Weekly tickets (excluding Sunday) 1s 6d (7½p) men, 1s 0d (5p) boys from Newport Pagnell.

From Linford the charge was 1s 0d (5p) for both. Actual numbers travelling at the time of acquisition by the LNWR were:-

Newport to Wolverton 370 men, 121 boys;
Linford to Wolverton 92 men, 8 boys.

A daily train of nearly 600 is a patronage that many minor branch lines would consider fruitful indeed! It gained the company by £38 16s 0d (£38.80p).

When Newport Pagnell station opened for passenger business in 1867 it must have had a decidedly truncated look. A through platform leading to a viaduct over the Wolverton Road. Had track been laid down on this latter section and the line to Olney opened this structure would have needed modification at some time. The plans for the NPR were for a double track cross-country route to Wellingborough with train working beyond. If heavy freight trains traversed this section it would require some deft teamwork between goods guard and driver on loose coupled trains. Some planned gradients on the Olney extension had two 1 in 60 and two 1 in 80 for three miles, positively alpine!

As matters transpired the line was never put to the test and after the purchase by the LNWR the prospect of extension was buried forever. Or so it seemed until the redoubtable local interests resurrected the idea with a roadside tramway of standard gauge in 1887.

This proposal was promulgated under the 1870 Tramways Act which

40

proved to be its Achilles heel. This Act, that was amended later, did not contain powers of compulsory purchase which is incredibly slip-shod in view of this being a crucial factor in all the contentious world of railway building since the 1830's.

Guilelessly the promoters drew up their plans to run from the station and along the Wolverton Road, over North Bridge, Lathbury Bridge, Sherrington Bridge and a mile further. Curving at the road junction to Sherrington village it continues up the village street and on to Emberton reaching a road junction from south-west of Emberton and along the main street. At Olney it passes over the Mill Race and along Bridge Street, along the High Street forming a triangle in the market place before continuing up the High Street and ending with a terminus outside 'The Castle' public house on the junction of Dartmouth Road and Station Road, also close to the 'Queen Hotel, a distance of 5¼ miles. It was to be steam operated on a 4' 8½" gauge with flanged wheels. In effect probably identical in concept to the Stony Stratford Tramway which was in fact built and ran for 39 years.

The Olney Tramway did not as mentioned fare so well. It appears that a landowner at Emberton acted out of spite and stopped its progress.

Ordnance Survey of 1878 with later railway additions shows some lines of Tramway running into the station yard so it would seem that some of the line was indeed built. No evidence had arisen to suggest that any traction was put into service along these rails. Communications between the towns remained therefore in the hands of road services. The country's first motor bus service began on this route in 1898.

In the terms set out by the LNWR for purchase of the NPR they include a cost for the demolition of the viaduct at Newport Pagnell. This they did not do. In the Minutes of the LNWR Traffic Committee instructions are entered for the boarding up of the arches and flooring the ground with sleepers so as to increase accommodation for grain traffic. From photographic evidence this was obviously done and utilized as such until is complete demolition circa 1879.

There were in fact a number of improvements that the LNWR put in hand. In 1877 a cattle pen and horse landing was constructed. In 1883 a ground frame was installed on the platform to work the station signals and points. Two new signal posts, keys to lock points and catch points. The approach to Newport Pagnell was protected by a 'home' signal which was 'fixed', trains entered the station beneath a shorter 'calling on' arm fixed beneath it. At the end of the platform there was an illuminated 'stop' signal that controlled entrance into the goods yard. For the return journey there was an 'up' starter beyond the platform but no signal for entering the single road steam shed. There were signals at Bradwell and Linford for stopping trains which did not exist in later years leaving nothing until the Wolverton 'home'. Provided the branch was worked according to regulations there was no danger of collision. This was on the one engine in steam principle with train staff. Intermediate signalling was probably removed with the introduction of the train staff which came into use on the branch in 1905. This was round and coloured Red, it enabled all the few sidings on the branch to be locked by the staff, Wolverton triangle, Bradwell Siding with the line from the station into the goods yard locked by Annett's Key. On the 1 March 1873 absolute block working came into operation between Bletchley and Stafford.

The single road locomotive steam shed was brought from Leighton Buzzard to Newport Pagnell in 1889. This had the effect of establishing the depot as a sub-shed of Bletchley, staffed by a driver and fireman living in the town. A third member of staff was employed as a 'lighter up'. This could have been a semi-retired railwayman or someone in a supernumerary role. His would be the chore to trudge through early winter mornings of the town streets at 4.00 am to ensure that the engine would be primed with a head of steam for the first train at 5.30 am. Important to the Wolverton works as it ensured that over 400 men reached work on time. It is very likely that the engine would be simmering on a low fire overnight. A second workmen's train was at 7.40 am this was probably for clerical staff. The fare was 4d (2p) from Newport and 3d (1p) from great Linford.

On 1 January 1916 the old shed, that was probably all timber, was totally consumed by a disastrous fire that not only destroyed it but badly damaged the branch engine, a 4 ft 6 in 2-4-2 tank No. 889.

The replacement shed was a decidedly unflattering structure, made of wood and galvanised iron. This shed remained in use until the depot's closure on 13 June 1955. Actual rails into the shed were removed on 20 September 1957. The building was very likely to have been demolished shortly before or after.

With the filling in of the canal basin and the goods yard being built on the land the railway was then in a position of taking over the former business. This was as mentioned previously not as plentiful as had been hoped. Coal was undoubtedly the main commodity with tonnages of 7,269 for 1874 the final complete year of the NPR.

An Agreement for a private Corn Mill siding in the yard; at right angles to the two goods sidings using a 12 ft turntable to their own loading shed of Messrs Price and Goff, was drawn up in December 1870 and came into use in the following February.

Another and possibly earlier siding did not enter the goods yard at all but diverted from the station before the platform crossing over the shed line and out of the station altogether by 146 yards to reach Hives & Sons building. This was in 1885 taken over by Francis Coales & Son. For the information of the working of this private siding I am indebted to Mr John Coales FSA who describes it thus:-

'We had a flour mill which was powered by a 96 h.p. Crossley Gas Engine (now in store at Stacey Hill Museum, Wolverton) for which we had a gas producer plant. This used a mixture of coke and anthracite which came in trucks (railway ones!) down into our yard.

After my grandfather died my father expanded the production of animal compound feed which entailed extension of the buildings *over* the railway tracks. Pre-1939 we used to receive a considerable amount of imported raw materials by rail; the full trucks were left at the top of the line, behind the passenger station, then our foreman would take the brake off each one as he was ready to unload it and it came down by gravity; surely a practice that would not be allowed today!

We also sold salt and from time to time we would receive a yellow Saxa Salt truck which came from the salt mines in Cheshire. It was the practice at Newport to do the Goods shunting in the morning – there was no passenger train to Wolverton between about 9 am and 1 pm so when the 9 am train returned the engine did all the goods shunting. Then a different (?larger) engine came about 2 pm bringing full wagons and taking away those which were empty or had been loaded at Newport. We used to send away quantities of grain and also flour. After nationalisation this almost ceased because it took about a month to get a quotation of price for a consignment; in pre-nationalisation days one walked across to the goods office where the clerk could tell you the rate. During the morning the shunting engine would come down into our yard to collect trucks. This was an event of great excitement as smoke and steam would come into the part over the lines through the trap doors used for hoisting raw materials out of the trucks.

43

Just behind the passenger station building was a short line that terminated in a ramp. Here Messrs Salmons & Sons (now Aston Martin Lagonda) would load their cars onto special trucks.'

Some Aston Martin cars were loaded by this ramp in front of the station into open ended vans. Salmons brought their chassis by rail to Newport then hauled them by one horse power to the works in Tickford.

An amusing piece of sarcasm appeared in the Newport Pagnell Gazette on 27 January 1872 complaining about the muddy state of the road leading up to the station. This appears to have been a problem since the station opened and suggests that there was little or no drainage at all on this road. This is often a problem for marginal strips of land that fall just outside the liabilities of separate authorities. The correspondent goes on '..... if nothing is done the making of stilts will become an important local industry.' One can well imagine what the cartoonist Heath-Robinson would have drawn from that statement. With the graphic interpretation of dozens of local townspeople walking back and forth from the station on stilts! On a more serious note there had been a great deal of protest about the station site after the opening enthusiasm had cooled. A photograph illustrated in this book shows the liability to serious flood which became common in building during the 19th century when areas liable to flood became exacerbated by new earthworks and installations.

There was a serious petition to the LNWR to get the station resited in 1887. However forcefully the point was made it did not prevail.

CHAPTER TWO

Wolverton

The original village of Wolverton dates back to the neolithic age and appropriate to mans first effective use of tools it was about 4 miles west of the centre of the existing town. From the time of the building of the main line in 1838 when it had a population of 417 the name has become synonymous with the great railway works. Also with what is regarded to be the best social effects of the Industrial Revolution. One hundred years later the population had become seven thousand.

The area had no topographical claim to be so chosen as a site for the new locomotive works of the London & Birmingham Railway other than simply being placed conveniently half way between the two points, becoming first a locomotive changing point. But with the development of Wolverton and the later expansion of Bletchley as an operating centre a few miles south, this area of north Bucks became one of the major concentrations of railway business in the country. In a similar way that mere villages became household names with large works concentrations like Crewe in Cheshire and the small town of Horwich in Lancashire, Wolverton became a railway capital.

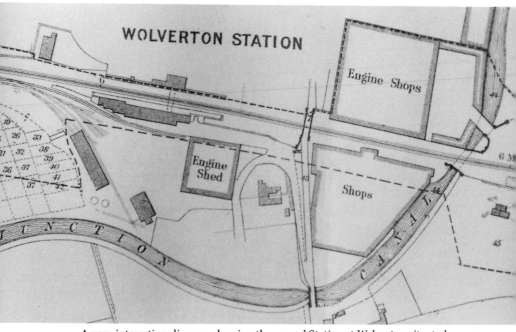

WOLVERTON STATION

Engine Shops

Engine Shed

Shops

A very interesting diagram showing the second Station at Wolverton situated south of the Stratford Road bridge. This is the station with which the Newport Pagnell Railway was connected. Believed to have been resited by the London & Birmingham Railway c1845. It lasted until the new deviation station in 1881. The rails of the NPR are not included on this plan, but comparison with the plan on (p.55) will give an indication of the arrangement. North roadbridge, restricted by the Grand Junction Canal is the original locomotive workshops, very modest compared with what was to follow. The bridge to carry rails into the works appears to have been constructed, as yet awaiting rails.

Buckinghamshire County Record Office (PUC 166).

The history of Wolverton works has been chronicled very effectively by Bill West in his book *The Railwaymen — Wolverton.* Here it is relevant insomuch as it concerns the branch but some historical perspective is required. The Company acquired 8 acres of land at Wolverton in 1837. With the opening of the locomotive works in 1838 the area was firmly in the hands of a railway that was in itself very much in development. The original works was lauded as the Grand Central works but was a very modest plant compared with what was to follow. Bound on one side by the Stratford Road and the other by a curve of the Grand Junction Canal and of course the railway itself. Land had been purchased from the Radcliffe Trustees that owned most of the land in the area. To provide habitation for

Webb Coal tank 7773 waiting to leave Wolverton with the 12.15pm Saturday workmen's on the 18 of may 1946. The LNWR engines replaced the NPR engines in 1875. Two locos hired by them from Jas Taylor of Springfield, Whitmore, Nr Stafford.

H C Casserley

their employees the Company built a number of streets adjoining. Along them the familiar blocks of terraced housing, 84 houses in the first stage in 1840. At that time the works was employing 400 people. In June 1840 the L&B bought 14 acres more land which they had built over by 1847.

With the formation of the London & North Western Railway in June 1846 the financial strength existed to develop Wolverton on a great scale.

The LNWR applied to the Radcliffe Trustees for more land in 1858 this allowed the works to be expanded considerably and within two years had increased their workforce to 2,000 men.

After a shaky period in the latter years of the 1840's railway development was moving apace throughout the 1850's and 60's and the LNWR forever conscious of what was happening at Derby (Midland) and Paddington (Great Western) seemed determined to stay in the forefront. In 1860-1 the Radcliffe Trustees appeared less willing than hitherto to sell more land. The Company then bought and developed land at New Bradwell where 150 workers cottages were built. The population of New

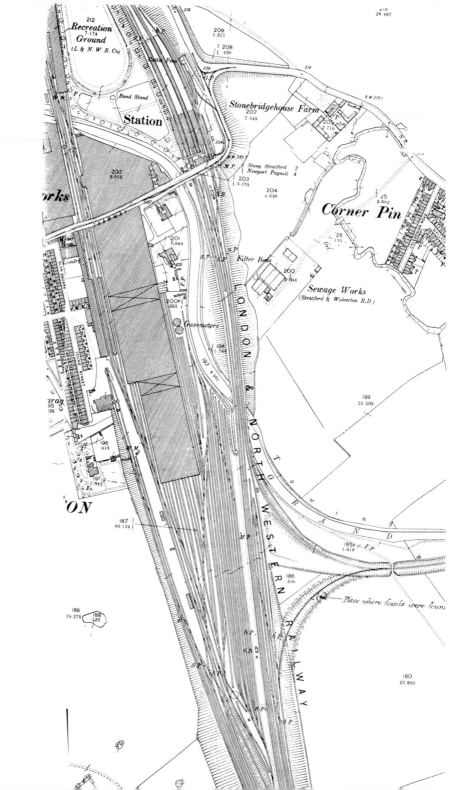

Station approach at Wolverton late summer of 1914. Older men look thoughtfully on as the young men, many from the works, join the Army and face the ensuing battles of the Somme. A special train took the men to Cowley Barracks, Oxford to join the Oxon and Bucks Regiment. Beneath their feet, are the rails of the Wolverton and Stony Stratford Tramway.

Wolverton Archeological Society.

Bradwell increased dramatically between 1861-1871 from 1,658 to 2,409. The number of houses rising from 233 to 506.

By 1864-66 the Trustees must have relented as the Company put in hand a scheme to virtually double the size of the works with carriage body and repair shops, finishing shop, forges and foundry, axle shop, timber stores, sawmill and paint shops. Also a school for signalmen was established.

Wolverton, fifty-two miles from Euston. The triangle of the Newport Pagnell branch and the connection with Wolverton station. An interesting connection with the Stony Stratford Tramway this entered the yard of the station alongside the Newport Pagnell branch platform. The area was fortunate in the provision of triangles, there was one at Bedford and another at Northampton. Survey of 1900 period.

Ordnance Survey

Men leaving the Works at Wolverton c1913. The centre of the picture is dominated by one of the huge double-deck Tramway coaches. By this time the Works employed 5,000 men, at the peak. They started work at 6 am and continued with a pause at 8.15 until 9 for breakfast. Lunch came at 1, until 2; the day finally ended at 5.30pm. Their week also included Saturday from 6 am until 12 noon. Note the two bowler hatted 'gaffers' striding out from the bottom left hand corner of the picture. In front of them a line of makeshift carrier carts with boys. They used these to bring hot dinners to their fathers and relatives in the works from Bradwell.

Bob Ayres Collection

Wolverton Station buildings on 26 August 1961. The mostly timber 'chalet' style structure dates from its opening of the deviation on 1 August 1882 it did not manage to survive the effects of the late twentieth century and was demolished in the summer of 1991.

John H Meredith.

Such was the need to reorganise the works area that the streets of Walker Street, Cooke Street, Garnet Street and Gas Street newly built were summarily demolished. But for many years the paved street patterns remained on the floors of the workshops that enclosed them.

What in effect was taking place was the beginning of corporate planning in railway manufacture. Early railways had been put together in a very piecemeal way as would be expected of such developments of limited experience. By the 1860's there were men of organising ability and sufficient experience to know what was needed. The LNWR saw itself as a national concern, a railway empire that would be wholly self sufficient. Wolverton was being organised into something that motor car manufacturers have received the credit for, mass production, but for the LNWR it was an entire transport system from its nuts and bolts to its station buildings.

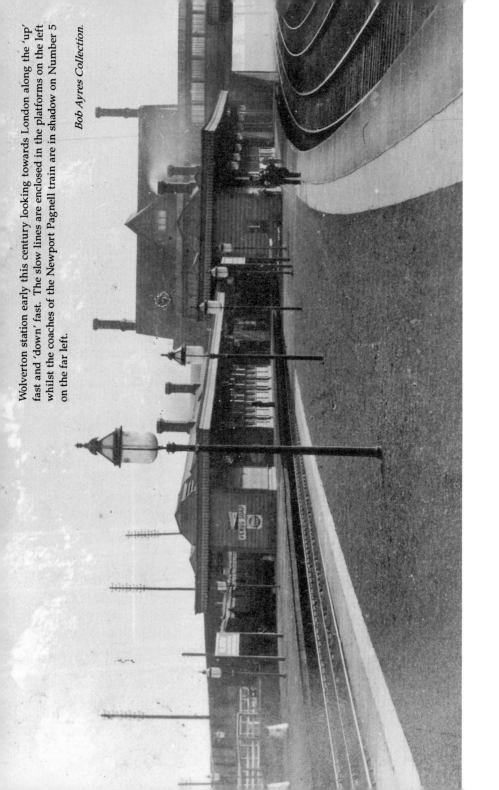

Wolverton station early this century looking towards London along the 'up' fast and 'down' fast. The slow lines are enclosed in the platforms on the left whilst the coaches of the Newport Pagnell train are in shadow on Number 5 on the far left.

Bob Ayres Collection.

Not a very clear print but included for its comparison with the photograph on page 4. Of all the views from Blue Bridge south of the works showing the junction it is the only one that has come to light showing an 18" Goods shunting the works 'down' sidings.

Bob Ayres Collection

Supporting pillars of this great undertaking was the former Grand Junction works at Crewe and Wolverton.

Many of the employees of the works came from Lancashire and Birmingham, the effects of this growth must have totally drained local agriculture. Fifty years of expansion to 1910 saw the peak of 5,000 employees covering 80 acres of land.

Amongst all the changes during that time the most significant was first of all moving all the locomotive building and maintenance to Crewe and centralizing all the carriage construction and repair at Wolverton, this took place in 1862.

The removal of the locomotive building to Crewe was not without its social effects. Understandably some trades were specifically intended for locomotive building purposes, boilersmiths, and various engineering

The sunlight reveals a part of Wolverton station that is often in shadow. A building that lasted until 1991. The Bletchley Super D 48953 ended her days thirty years before in 1961. It is possible that she is on the Newport sidings to pick up; or as in some cases on a running in turn from Bletchley shed. After WWII the daily freight duty to Newport Pagnell was mainly handled by exLYR 0-6-0's. The signals reading from left to right are, Newport starter, 'up' slow, 'up' fast.

H C Casserley

fitters. It is therefore interesting to comprehend this change in terms of decrease and increase in local population.

	1861	1871	Decrease
Great Brickhill	590	566	24
Little Brickhill	423	291	132
Bow Brickhill	546	468	78
Woughton-on-the-Green	314	273	41
Great Linford	557	468	89
Cosgrove	776	646	130
	1861	**1871**	**Increase**
Bradwell	1658	2409	751
Wolverton	2370	2804	534

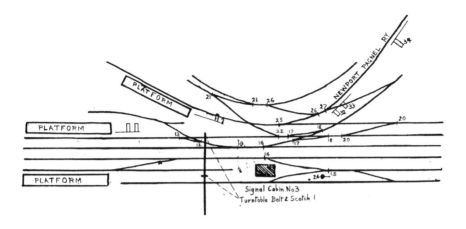

A copy from a diagram from a Board of Trade report of 1876 concerning an accident at Wolverton. The interesting revelation is the exact disposition of the platforms at Wolverton to cater for the branch. This complex and fragmented arrangement implies that the branch was tacitly conceded to by the LNWR. The Newport Pagnell Railway had only ceased to exist twelve months prior to this diagram. This was the second Wolverton station, south of the Stratford Road. Quadrupling in the late seventies and the deviation in 1881 would sweep all of this away. The branch at this junction was 3 miles 6 furlongs and 9 chains.

Geoffrey Webb, BoT Report

A marked contrast in socio-industrial change is the comparison with Little Brickhill losing a third of its population compared to Bradwell which saw well over a third increase! The figures are taken from the Census of England and Wales of 1871.

The other significant factor was the quadrupling of the main line throughout in 1879. This was like building the railway over again with stations and junctions on a much grander scale.

By the 7 February 1877 contracts had been completed for the widening of the railway between Bletchley and Roade. Also for the construction of a new railway from Roade to Northampton (this was the preferred alternative to the Bletchley, Newport Pagnell, Northampton Railway of 1859). Further land was at that time being purchased for the railway from Northampton to Rugby, thereby annexing Northampton into the system proper. Work began on all of this in 1878 with special problems at Wolverton with the station having once been moved from out of the path of the expanding works to south of the Stratford Road and being found

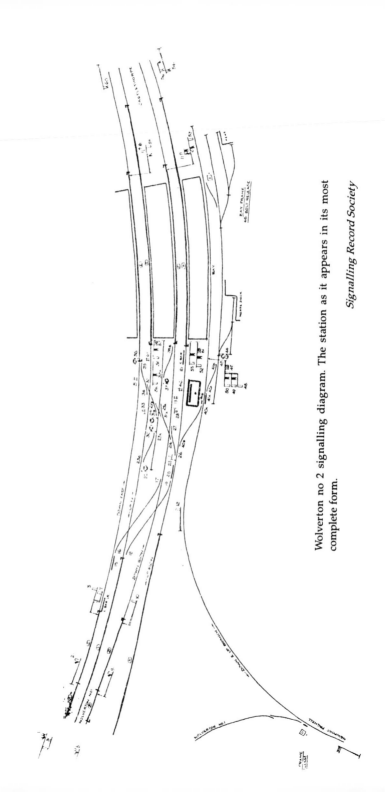

Wolverton no 2 signalling diagram. The station as it appears in its most complete form.

Signalling Record Society

Wolverton station 31 July 1964 Ivatt 41222 on the 'Newport Nobby'. Note the cattle dock on the right and LMS concrete loading gauge. Behind the usual two coaches are two others with another engine. It is possible that two extra coaches are being attached, if that is the case, this is probably the evening workmen's train.

K C H Fairey.

for a second time to be in the way. The answer was to move the entire main line and station east. What came to be known as the Wolverton deviation. Resulting not only in a new station but burrowing junctions for the works exit line. Part of all the new works was a new bridge (176) over the canal for access to the works.

The movement of the station consequently altering the branch to Newport Pagnell with it.

This third and final Wolverton station was opened for business on 1 August 1882 for passengers. Goods and minerals had been running on the deviation for twelve months previous.

About 1902-3 a significant alteration to the junction of the branch was the connection of a southern line junction with the main line. This effectively created a triangle which was utilized for turning the royal train that was permanently held at Wolverton. This third part of a triangle appears on the working timetable for the first time in February 1903.

The Newport Pagnell train about to leave its platform at Wolverton on the 5 September 1964 behind Ivatt 41222 2-6-2T.

L Hanson

A backward glance as 'Newport Nobby' departs from Wolverton on 29 August 1964. Electrification suggests a comparatively recent view, but this scene is now so bleakly reduced. Gone the train, the signalbox and semaphores and most recent of all — 1991, the station buildings.

Peter Baughan.

A superb lyrical study of the LNWR 0-6-2 coal Tank rounding the curve from Wolverton and the main line running across the background of the picture. The triangular arrangement completed with the addition of the south curve in 1903 is clearly seen. Within a very short time the push-pull set will be arriving at Bradwell station. Listed in the Working Appendix in 1879 was a Signal Box called 'Bradwell' to the right of the place where the train is passing.

W J S Meredith

L. & N. W. R.]   3.—Cheddington and Aylesbury Branch.

Week Days.																		Sundays.					
EUSTON ....dep.	6 10	7 20	9 10	11 5	1220	1 45	3b 0	5 0	6 10	7 10	....	....	....	....	9 0	2 45	....	—	—	—	—
CHEDDINGTON n	7 40	8 42	1040	1240	1 40	3 15	4 48	6 0	7 20	8 35	9 36	....			1024	4 40		—	—	—	—
MARSTON GATE n	7 47	8 49	1047	1247	1 47	3 22	4 55	6 7	7 27	8 42	9 37	....			1032	4 47		—	—	—	—
AYLESBURY — arr.	7 57	8 57	1055	1255	1 57	3 30	5 3	6 15	7 35	8 50	9 43	—	—		1042	4 57		—	—	—	—

Week Days.								A	W						Sundays.				W Runs on Wednesdays only.
AYLESBURY ....dep.	7 5	8 12	9 10	12 0	2 10	2 15	3 55	4 0	5 30	6 50	8 0	9 0	....	7 25	10 0	5 5	....	—	A Does not run on Wednesdays.
MARSTON GATE n	7 15	8 21	9 19	12 9	2 19	2 26	4 4	4 9	5 39	6 59	8 9	9 9	....	7 35	10 9	5 15	....	—	b On Saturdays leaves Euston at 3 10.
CHEDDINGTON ......arr.	7 22	8 30	9 95	1215	1 26	2 33	4 10	4 15	5 45	6 45	8 15	9 15	....	7 42	1015	5 22	....	—	* Saturdays only.
EUSTON — n	8 40	9 35	1095	1 50	3a50	4	5 6	5	6 5	—	1023	....	....	9 35	1245	7 40	—	—	

L. & N. W. R.]   4.—Wolverton and Newport Pagnell Branch.—Week Days only.

			N	B		X				N	B					
EUSTON ....dep.	7 10	....	8 35	....	1010	1010	1225	....	2 45	3c 0	3 5	6 10	8 0	7 10	....	....
WOLVERTON — n	8 30	9 15	10 0	....	1146	1210	2 30	3 35	4 20	5 45	6 55	7 50	9 45	9 55	....	....
BRADWELL .... n	8 32	9 17	1011	11 0	1151	1273	2 33	3 38	4 23	5 48	6 66	7 53	....	....	....	....
GREAT LINFORD — n	8 37	9 22	1016	1114	1156	1218	2 38	3 43	4 28	5 53	7 0	7 58	A	A	....	....
NEWPORT PAGNELL arr.	8 42	9 27	1020	1119	12 1	1223	2 43	3 48	4 33	5 58	7 5	8 3	9 56	10 6	....	....

							X								
NEWPORT PAGNELL dep.	5 30	7 30	8 30	9 40	1040	1040	1196	1 5	2 10	3 55	5 20	6 20	7 25	8 45	....	A Calls when required.
GREAT LINFORD n	5 35	7 35	8 55	9 44	1044	1130	1 10	2 14	4 0	5 25	6 24	....	8 50	....	—	B Does not run on Saturdays. B Runs on Saturdays only.
BRADWELL .... n	....	7 42	9 0	9 49	1049	1135	1 15	3 21	4 5	5 36	6 29	....	8 55	....	—	X Runs on Wednesdays and Saturdays only.
WOLVERTON — arr.	5 41	7 45	9 2	9 52	1053	1138	1 18	3 25	4 8	5 36	6 32	7 35	8 58	....	—	b On Saturdays leaves Euston at 3 10. † Not on Saturdays.
EUSTON .... n	....	9 35	1010	12 0	1245	....	2 55	5 15	....	7 30	8 20	9 50	1110	....	—	‡ 1st & 3rd Class only.

Extract from Bradshaw's Railway Guide in 1908. The Aylesbury — Cheddington and Newport — Wolverton Branches ran along very similar lines but the latter never seemed to justify a Sunday service.

Bill Simpson Collection

OXFORD & BLETCHLEY BRANCH.

1st, 2nd, and 3rd Class by all Trains.

From Oxford.	WEEK DAYS										SUNDAYS	
Oxford	7 50											
Islip	8 0											
Bicester	8 12											
Launton	8 19											
Clayton	8 33											
Verney Junction	8 40											
Winslow	8 46											
Swanbourne	9 1											
Bletchley	9 15											
London—Euston	10 35											

To Oxford.	WEEK DAYS									SUNDAYS	
London—Euston											
Bletchley											
Swanbourne											
Winslow											
Verney Junction											
Clayton											
Launton											
Bicester											
Islip											
Oxford											

BANBURY & BUCKINGHAM BRANCH.

1st, 2nd, and 3rd Class by all Trains.

From Banbury.	WEEK DAYS					
Banbury						
Farthinghoe						
Brackley						
Buckingham						
Verney Junction						
Winslow						
Swanbourne						
Bletchley						
London—Euston						

To Banbury.	WEEK DAYS						SUNDAYS	
London—Euston								
Bletchley								
Swanbourne								
Winslow								
Verney Junction								
Buckingham								
Brackley								
Farthinghoe								
Banbury								

BEDFORD & HITCHIN BRANCH.

1st and 3rd Class by all trains. No trains on Sundays.

To Hitchin.			
Bedford			
Cardington			
Southill			
Shefford			
Henlow			
Hitchin			
London—King's†			

From Hitchin.			
London—King's†			
Hitchin			
Henlow			
Shefford			
Southill			
Cardington			
Bedford			

Newport & Wolverton.

From											
Newport											
Bradwell											
Wolverton											

From											
Wolverton											
Bradwell											
Newport											

Timetable of trains on the Newport Pagnell branch and other district services in 1883. The 'down' 5.30am, 7.45am, and 'up' 8.42am and 6-48pm were 'parliamentaries'. Trains charging 1 penny a mile to enable working class people to move about in days when railways were very expensive.

Sid Sellers Collection

Between Wolverton and Bradwell the motor train still running with the LNWR motor coach in this view taken in the 1950's.

Ken Nunn Collection/LCGB

Against the background of Wolverton works Ivatt 2-6-2 tank lifts the Newport Pagnell bound train along the north face of the triangle. Having crossed over the Grand Junction Canal on the bridge in the distance.

Ken Nunn Collection/LCGB

Rural Bucks on the last day of July 1964. Ivatt 41222 has left Wolverton and is on the Wolverton side of the triangle approaching the footbridge that carries the footpath from Old Bradwell to Wolverton. The bridge was completed in April 1865 and removed in the late 1970's.

K C H Fairey.

CHAPTER THREE

Great Linford and Bradwell

Station buildings on the line could not be described as anything more than stout and basic. In the rectangular block at Newport Pagnell was the booking office and single waiting room adjoining urinal, WC, store and lamp room. The support of the canopies on the platform side and the entrance side was unusual, instead of columns they were suspended with cable ties to the chimney stacks. This enabled the limited space of the platform to be completely clear of obstruction. Comparison with Great Linford and Bradwell is easy to make on photographs as both appear as scaled down versions of same building without canopies.

Linford became Great Linford on the timetable of 1884 (28 July 1893). In view of the heavy use of the canal there it is surprising that no siding was ever needed by local merchants. Presumably coal supplies were

Good view of the former LMS push and pull unit at Great Linford in the early sixties with the Ivatt 2-6-2 tank in charge. Confirmed at 3.20 pm on a summer's afternoon by the station clock. This is a little odd as there was no train timed to be at Great Linford at this time or near it in the timetable.

Stephen Summersen.

Rail level view of Great Linford station in July 1959. When the line became part of the LNWR a stationmaster's house was built at Linford. Information for modellers, the platform is 264ft long.

H C Casserley

Banbury, Wolverton, and Newport Pagnell.—L. and N. W.											
STATIONS.	a.m.	a.m.	p.m.	p.m.	p.m.	STATIONS.	a.m.	a.m.	p.m.	p.m.	p.m.
BANBURY ..	7 40	9 50	2 20	4 25	7 15	Newprt. Pgnl.	7 45	10 15	2 35	4 50	8 20
Bletchley ..dep.	10 20	11 23	4 12	6 30	8 50	Wolverton ar.	8 0	10 27	2 50	5 2	8 32
Wolverton ..arr.	10 30	11 33	4 22	6 40	9 1	Wolverton dep.	8 5	11 2	3 19	5 41	8 34
Wolverton dp.	11 5	12 35	4 25	6 48	9 10	Bletchley ..arr.	8 18	11 15	3 31	5 52	8 50
Newprt. Pgnl.	11 20	12 47	4 37	7 0	9 22	BANBURY ..	9 40	1 40	5 38	7 42	10 25

plentifully supplied by the canal which could well be a contributing factor to the less than total success of the Newport Pagnell Railway unable to wean customers away from the canal. A station master's house was built at Linford in 1878.

Bradwell, which, to be admitted is much closer to Wolverton had the only private siding on the line apart from Newport Pagnell. Wylie's Lime Works Siding was opened as a result of an agreement dated 4 August 1870. A very severely curved siding of 161 yards back towards Wolverton.

A notable feature of Bradwell was the capacious water tank house and water tank, interestingly located as the only supply of water on the branch, water is drawn from a system put in by the LNWR, from a spring

A train's eye view of Great Linford Station. The buildings on the branch were solid brick, without frills, ideal modelling subjects. the post mounted lamp and the hand water pump are interesting touches. This view on 29 August 1964.

Peter E Baughan.

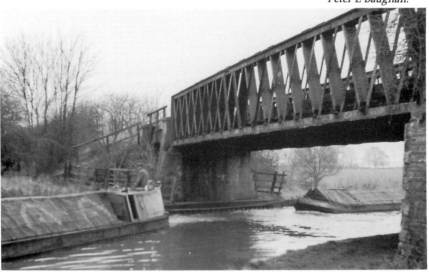

Without doubt the most significant engineering feature on the branch was the iron lattice bridge that carries it over the Grand Junction Canal at Linford, the summit of the line.

Ray Bailey.

A Fairburn tank enters Great Linford proudly displaying 'South Midlands Railtour' of the LCGB on the 17 of October 1964. The engine 42105 is from Bletchley.

P Waylett

near Wolverton. With the further curiosity of it being supplied to a London & Birmingham (Bury) design water column dated 1847 and built by Curtis & Kennedy. This was on a square tapered base with a fluted shaft to 2/3 way then curved over at a right angle at the top with a hanging canvas 'bag'. The room of the water tank house became a lamp room on the 18 October 1882 when the lamp room on the station became a ladies WC.

The Lime Kilns were situated alongside the siding in the side of a cutting that ran from the railway to the canal. This enabled Wylie to utilise both transport systems. A roadway to the top of the cutting enabled the limestone to be fed into the top of the kilns. Forty tons of coal were brought in and 30 tons of lime sent out each week. Work seems to have ceased shortly before the First World War. What seems a reasonable

Between Bradwell and Great Linford 41222 passes the place where on Monday 8 January, 1872 a locomotive cylinder head blew off. There were no casualties.

Peter Waylett

NEWPORT PACNELL BRANCH.

LEAVE	A.M	A.M	A.M	A.M	P.M	P.M	P.M	P.M	P.M	P.M	LEAVE	A.M	A.M	A.M	P.M	P.M	P.M	P.M	P.M	P.M	P.M
Newport	5 30	7 45	8 53	1030	1 40	2 0	...	5 20	6 10	8 15	London (Euston)	7 15	8 0	1010	1215	...	2 45	3 15	5	9 8	10
Linford	5 35	7 50	8 58	1034	*	3	4	...	5 25	6 15	8 20	Wolverton, depart	8 35	1010	1136	2 20	...	4	10 5	45	6 409	47
Bradwell	...	7 55	9 3	1039	1 50	3	0	WS 5 30	6 20	8 25	Bradwell	8 37	1014	1139	2 23	WS	4	13 5	48	6 43	...
Wolverton	5 41	7 58	9 5	1043	1 53	3	13	...	5 33	6 23	8 28	Linford	8 42	1019	1144	2 28	...	4	18 5	53	6 48	*
Euston	...	9 35	1025	1210	3 45	4	45	...	7 50	...	1015	Newport Pagnell	8 47	1023	1149	2 33	...	4	23 5	58	6 53 9	58

WS.—Additional Trains run on Wednesdays and Saturdays.   No Sunday Trains.   * Stop by Signal.

Branch trains with London connections in October 1894.

Sid Sellers Collection

68

Bill Simpson Collection

NEWPORT PAGNELL BRANCH—SINGLE LINE.

Train Staff Stations—WOLVERTON and NEWPORT PAGNELL.

Only one Engine, or two Engines coupled together, allowed on this Branch at the same time.

DOWN — Week Days / SUNDAYS

Distance from Wolverton (Miles)	Station	49 G'ds	50	51	52 Pass.	53 Pass.	54 Mixed	57 SO	58 SO	59 Pass.	61 Goods SO	62 SO	63 Pass.	66 Pass.	67 Pass.	69 Pass.	70 Pass.	71 Pass.	73 Eng. & Break (SUNDAYS)
			a.m.		a.m.	a.m.	a.m.	a.m.	a.m.	p.m.	p.m.	p.m.	p.m.	p.m.	p.m.	p.m.	p.m.	p.m.	a.m.
	Wolverton ... dep.		6 30	...	8 15	9 5	9 50	11 0	11 17	12 15	1 30	1 35	3 20	4 25	5 45	7 15	8 35	9 45	7 57
1	Bradwell ...		X	...	8 19	9 9	9 54	...	11 21	12 19	1 45	...	3 24	4 29	5 49	7 19	8 39	9 49	...
2¼	Great Linford ...		...	...	8 24	9 14	9 59	...	11 26	12 29	...	1 44	3 29	4 34	5 59	7 24	8 44	9 54	...
3¾	NEWPORT PAGNELL arr.		6 50	...	8 28	9 18	10 2	11 10	11 30	12 33	2 0	...	3 33	4 38	6 3	7 28	8 48	9 58	8 7

UP — Week Days / SUNDAYS

Distance from Newport Pagnell (Miles)	Station	75 Light Engine	76 Pass.	78 Pass.	79 Pass.	81 Pass.	84 Goods	87 Pass.	88 Pass. SO	89 Goods Mixed SO	90	92 Pass.	93 Pass.	96 Pass.	97 Pass.	99 Milk (SUNDAYS)
		a m	a.m.	a.m.	a.m.	a.m.	a.m.	p.m.	p.m.	p.m.	p.m.	p.m.	p.m.	p.m.	p.m.	a.m.
	NEWPORT PAGNELL dep.	5 45	7 25	8 42	9 27	10 40	11 40	1 0	1 52	2 20	3 55	5 20	6 20	8 0	9 10	8 20
1½	Great Linford ...	...	7 32	8 46	9 31	10 44	...	1 5	1 56	...	4 0	5 25	6 24	8 4	9 15	...
2¼	Bradwell ...	...	7 39	8 51	9 36	10 49	...	1 10	2 1	...	4 5	5 30	6 29	8 9	9 20	...
3¾	Wolverton ... arr.	5 55	7 42	8 54	9 39	10 52	11 55	1 13	2 4	2 40	4 8	5 33	6 32	8 12	9 23	8 30

Working timetable for the branch in May 1909. Note the Sunday only run up the branch for the milk train.

Bill Simpson Collection

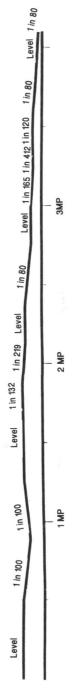

The gradient profile of the line rising to clear the Grand Junction Canal, (Grand Union Canal).

Gradient markers: Level — 1 in 100 — 1 MP — 1 in 100 — Level — 1 in 132 — Level — 1 in 219 — 2 MP — 1 in 80 — Level — 1 in 165 — 1 in 412 — 1 in 120 — 3MP — Level — 1 in 80 — 1 in 80 — Level

Bill Simpson

A concrete footbridge erected over the branch in the early 1960's.

Ray Bailey Collection.

certainty is that this would involve a 'trip' working by a goods engine, probably at the end of each working day.

It was subsequently used by coal merchants, Bradwell Mill itself had a steam engine for when the wind failed. There was also a substantial steam driven flour mill close by the station along the Old Bradwell Road which required substantial coal supplies and imported grain.

In the twenties the Anglo-Mexican Oil Co. had a depot alongside the siding.

Up to the final years of the branch Messrs. Goodmans Scrap Metal dealers had a yard at the siding and sent out wagons of scrap metal.

Bradwell early in the twentieth century with the attractive neat appearance of stations during the pre-grouping. The motive power, predictably and unmistakably one of the LNWR small tank engines. This view looking towards Wolverton.

Wolverton Archeological Society.

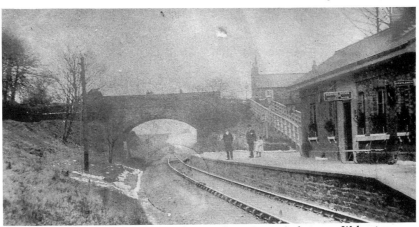

Looking down the line to the arriving or departing train between Wolverton and Bradwell, in the foreground. No specific date is available but it is likely to be before the First World War. The width of the bridge to the track clearly emphasizes the vaunted hopes of the Newport Pagnell Railway for a double track railway between Wolverton and Wellingborough or at the very least, to Olney.

Bob Ayres Collection

Although this photograph at Bradwell is during the period of the LMS it is perfectly LNWR and shows the two coach bogie set of the LNWR push-pull train.

W J S Meredith.

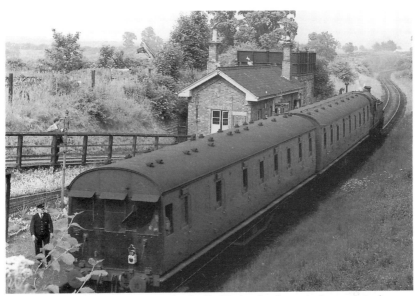

The ex-LMS Motor Train at Bradwell. Obviously the train is en route from Newport Pagnell to Wolverton as the driver is in the driving compartment of the motor coach. Clearly visible is the large water tank house built by the LNWR, this was supplied by a stream near the main line at Wolverton.

Stephen Summerson.

It is possible to imagine the casual conversation between the guard and the two ladies with youngsters in prams as he stands with the guards van door open and the train pauses at Bradwell on a journey to Newport Pagnell.

R K Blencowe.

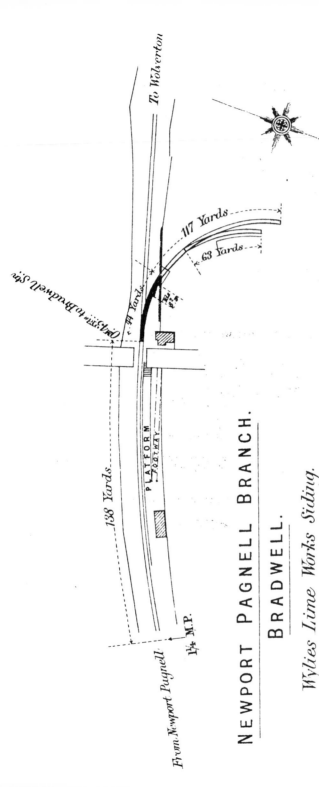

NEWPORT PAGNELL BRANCH.

BRADWELL.

Wylies Lime Works Siding.

To Wolverton

Over Bridge to Bradwell Str.

117 Yards

63 Yards

14 Yards

188 Yards

PLATFORM

FOOTWAY

1¼ M.P.

From Newport Pagnell

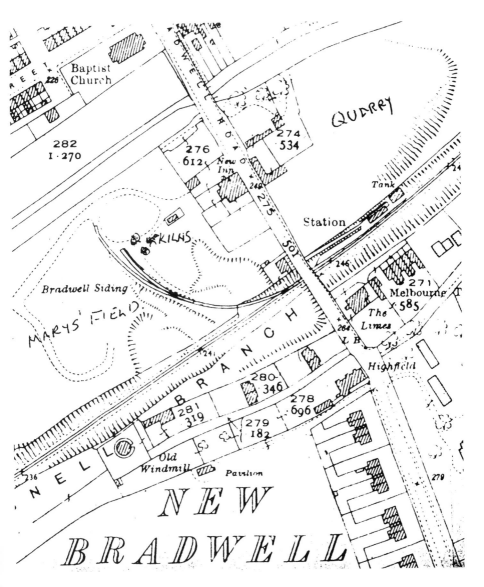

The station and siding at Bradwell. The building next to the bridge is the
Stationmaster's house

Ordnance Survey

Ground view of Bradwell station through the road bridge. The siding, formerly to Wylies Lime Works seen from a less common angle, August 1954. The building directly beneath the bridge is a pump house maintaining supplies down into the village of New Bradwell. Note also the lever frame for the siding as seen from the 'up' side to the 'down'.

K Barrow.

The siding at Bradwell seen from the Windmill.

Bill West

In its latter years the yard area alongside the siding at Bradwell was occupied by Goodmans Scrap Metal dealers. In this view of 22 August 1964 two 0-6-0 Saddle tanks have reached their melancholy end. Nothing is known by the author of their history but the photographer has thoughtfully included the following details. o/c HL 3138/15 & o/c AB 2138/41.

A Swain.

LICHFIELD T.V. TO LONDON (EUSTON) AND BRANCHES—continued.

STATIONS AND SIGNAL BOXES.			UP LINE	Lie-by Sidings and holding capacity		RUNAWAY CATCH POINTS.		Approximate Gradient. 1 in	ENGINE WHISTLES.					SPEED RESTRICTIONS.	
STATIONS AND SIGNAL BOXES, ETC.	Distance from place next above.			No. of Wagons.		WHERE SITUATE.	LINE.		UP.		DOWN.		TO	MILES PER HOUR.	
	Miles.	Yards.		Up Side.	Down Side.				Main, Fast or Passenger Line.	Slow or Goods Line.	Main, Fast or Passenger Line.	Slow or Goods Line.		UP.	DOWN.
NEWPORT PAGNELL STATION TO WOLVERTON No. 2.															
Newport Pagnell—Station	—	—												45	45
						Between Newport Pagnell and Wolverton									
Great Linford—Station	1	255													
Bradwell—Station	1	1130													
Wolverton—No. 2 *See page 60.*	1	375													
			Y			Curve leading from Newport Pagnell line to up slow main line								10	

35-TON BOGIE TANK WAGONS PROHIBITED FROM WORKING OVER CERTAIN LINES.

Bogie tank wagons with a carrying capacity of 35 tons must not work over the following lines :—

Garston Docks hydraulic drawbridge No. 5.
Whaley Bridge.
Newcastle (N.S.) goods yard.
Froghall (N.S.) wharf.
Holyhead mail pier jetty.
Anglesey Central line. Holland Arms to Amlwch.

Birkenhead portion of No. 2 bridge leading to Abbey Street coal yard.
Harborne Branch.
Leighswood Branch.
Wyken Branch.
Newport Pagnell Branch.

Restriction on the branch to 35 ton tank wagons from General Appendix to Working Time Table.

The view of the branch line on the left, though marginal shows in the distant, at Bradwell station on the other side of the bridge, a Saxby & Farmer signal, a slotted post semaphore utilizing the same lamp for the 'up' and 'down' semaphore arms. The arms are dropped to an angle of 45 degrees to show line clear in both directions.

Wolverton Archeological Society.

Bradwell in the 1950's looking towards Newport Pagnell. A notable feature in the station is the water column at the far end of the platform. This is a Bury design of the London & Birmingham Railway with the hints of the Company's appreciation of classical styling, with a pedestal base and fluted shaft.

Ken Nunn Collection/LCGB

Bradwell in the 1950's.

R.K. Blencowe.

Sidings connected with running lines and which are worked under special arrangements—continued.

Siding.	Position.	Particulars of working.
Triangle, points on branch ...	Wolverton	Ground frame, controlled by train staff.
N. Bradwell	Newport Pagnell branch	„ „ „ „
N. Coal yard	Newport Pagnell	Ground frame, Annett's key from ground frame at Wolverton end of platform.

Details of the Siding connection from General Appendix to Working Time Table.

Bradwell from the carriage window of the last day of service train 5 September 1964. The lady porter Mrs Walters, forces a thoughtful smile as she watches the train leave for Newport Pagnell. The sign behind her targets Transport Minister Ernest Marples with 'MARPLES MUST GO' an accurate observation of the power behind the remit of Doctor Beeching.

L Hanson

A Newport Pagnell bound train about to enter Bradwell Station. On the right is the only siding between Wolverton and Newport that was first installed for the use of Wylie's Lime Works in 1870, further along it can be seen the LNWR loading gauge. The notice alongside the Catch Points reads ' Engines must not pass this point' — but they did!

B W L Brooksbank.

Busy scene at Bradwell the 29 August 1964. The train is the 8.33 from Wolverton.

Peter Baughan

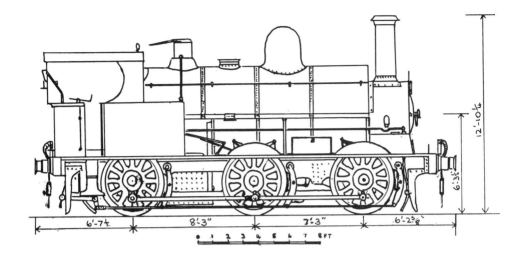

CHAPTER FOUR

Motive Power

A branch like Newport Pagnell is a natural choice for the tank engine, a short distance with regular stops at closely spaced stations. However, the opening of the branch pre-dates the appearance from Crewe of the known habitue of the line from the 1870's and 1880's so whatever hauled the trains for the first few years is a matter of conjecture.

Some early tank engines appeared in the 1860's an 0-4-2 WT No. 734 and a 2-2-2 ST No. 402 ran on hire to the NPR.

With the not unreasonable policy of the branches being operated by superannuated engines working out the post main line duties like ageing steeple chasers it seems reasonable to suppose that former L&B engines Bury 2-2-0 and 0-4-0 would not find four miles too taxing. With Trevithick 2-2-2's which are known to have been used on local branches being extremely likely. The lack of a turntable at Newport Pagnell would prove awkward for tender engines but here again not too great a test of endurance for four miles.

A photograph within the first years of the new British Railways ownership of the branch, on 10 April 1948. Apparently the branch was still being operated by a former LNWR 'Coal Tank' engine seen here as LMS 27561. The engine received the British Railways number of 58881 but was finally withdrawn in a very poor state in September 1950.

H C Casserley.

An ex-LNWR 2-4-2 46601 at Newport Pagnell in 1953. These engines were seen on all lines radiating from Bletchley. On this branch however they were not favoured alongside the more robust Coal Tanks. Shunting on the 1 in 80 into the goods yard was beyond their braking power with more than a very few wagons.

F G Cockman

What is known from photographic evidence is that the ubiquitous Webb 2-4-2 tanks did operate the branch and there is no reason to suppose that they did not from their introduction on the LNWR in the 1880's. The engine damaged, believed scrapped, in the shed fire of 1916 was a 'Motor Tank No. 889 which would be an obvious choice for the branch.

Up until its withdrawal in 1953 the larger cousin of the 4 ft 6 inch the 5 ft 6 inch No. 910 (LMS 6601 BR 4 6601) worked the branch for many years, along with No. 2146 (LMS 6666 BR 46666). The partnership died when the latter was withdrawn in 1948.

Occasionally the 2-4-2 tanks would be working the other branches, this branch alternated quite a great deal with the Aylesbury branch. On such occasions the branch engine would often be the Webb 'Coal Tank' No. 58887. This engine had not survived the rigours of time as the other engines and was in a worn out condition when it came to the line. The normal two coaches were accommodated well with careful handling on gradients of 1 in 80. But with six-coach trains the 58887 was hopelessly out of its depth. The regulator valve was never steam tight, so the engine had to be left with cylinder cocks open in addition to the normal requirement of brakes on and in mid gear. On a winter's day the loco was virtually hidden in a cloud of steam. The engine had really been living on borrowed time as it was withdrawn in March 1939 but brought back to service in 1940 for obvious reasons. It managed to attain a British Railways number in 1948 but finally passed unmourned by engine crews to the scrap heap in April 1955. It had then completed sixty-four years service.

Another 'Coal Tank' that did a term of service on the branch was No. 58881 (27561 LMS). This was withdrawn in September 1950.

Traction matters were much improved on the shorter branches when Bletchley received an allocation of brand new Ivatt (LMS) 2-6-2 tanks in 1949. The Aylesbury, Dunstable and Newport Pagnell branches were now assured of an engine that would be working well within its capacity. The

Bradshaw's Railway Guide in 1908.

Bill Simpson Collection

NEWPORT PAGNELL BRANCH—SINGLE LINE.

Train Staff Stations—WOLVERTON and NEWPORT PAGNELL.

Only one Engine, or two Engines coupled together, allowed on this Branch at the same time.

DOWN — Week Days only

Distance from Wolverton		1	2	3	4	5	6	7	8	9	10	11	12	13	14	15	16	17	18	19	20	21	22	23	24	25	26
		Gds.& Coal	Pass.		Pass.	Mixed Train.	Pass.	Pass.	Pass.	Pass.	Pass.	Pass. SO	G'ds.		Pass.	G'ds. SO	Pass. SO	Pass.		Pass.	Mixed Train.	Pass.	Pass.	Pass.	Pass.	Mixed Train.	
Miles		a.m.	a.m.		a.m.	a.m.	a.m.	a.m.	a.m.	noon	a.m.	p.m.	p.m.		p.m.	p.m.	p.m.			p.m.	p.m.	p.m.	p.m.	p.m.	p.m.	p.m.	
—	Wolverton ... dep.	6 20			8 30	9 15	10 15		11 7	12	12 0	12 10	1 30		2 20	3 35	3 40	4 16		5 45		6 32		7 40		9 50	
1¼	Bradwell ...	6 25			8 32	9 17	10 17		11 9	12	12 3	12 13			2 23	3 40	3 42	4 19		5 48		6 35		7 43		X	
2¼	Linford ...				8 37	9 22	10 22		11 14	12	12 8	12 18			2 28		3 48	4 24		5 53		6 39		7 48		10 1	
3¾	NEWPORT PAGNELL " arr.	6 50			8 42	9 27	10 27		11 19	12	12 13	12 23	1 40		2 33	C	3 53	4 29		5 58		6 43		7 53			

UP — Week Days only

Distance from Newport Pagnell		1	2	3	4	5	6	7	8	9	10	11	12	13	14	15	16	17	18	19	20	21	22	23	24	25	26
		Pass.	Pass.		Pass.	Mixed Train.	Pass.	Pass.	Pass.	Pass.		G'ds.	G'ds.		Mixed Train.	G'ds	Empty Coaches	Pass.		Pass.	Mixed Train.	G'ds.		Pass.	Pass.		
Miles		a.m.	a.m.		a.m.	a.m.	a.m.	a.m.		a.m.		p.m.	p.m.		p.m.			p.m.		p.m.	p.m.	p.m.		p.m.	p.m.		
—	NEWPORT PAGNELL dep.	5 30	7 30		8 53	9 45	10 40			11 26		1 5	1 55		3 15	S C	4 0	5 20		6 5	6 50			8 15			
1	Linford ... "	5 35	7 34		8 58	9 49	10 44			11 30		1 10			3 20			5 25		6 9				8 20			
2¼	Bradwell ... "		7 39		9 3	9 54	10 49			11 35		1 15			3 26		3 50	5 30		6 14				8 25			
3¾	Wolverton " arr.	5 41	7 42		9 5	9 57	10 53			11 38		1 18	2 5		3 30		3 55	5 33		6 17	7 0	7 0		8 28			

Working timetable for the branch of 1902. The busy daily shuttle of the 'Nobby' is evident. Note no 16 'up' train that will bring back the workmen's coaches on Saturday to be stored on Wolverton Sidings.

Peter Webber Collection

WOLVERTON and NEWPORT PAGNELL

Up.

Miles			Week Days only.
		mrn|mrn|mrn	aft|aft|aft|aft|aft|aft|aft
		S	S
—	Newport Pagnell ......dep.	7 28 10 8	2 11 4 51 7 4 5 22 6 10 7 40 9 38
1¼	Great Linford...... "	7 30 8 13 5 11 47	1 9 4 75 24 6 12 7 42 9 40
3	Bradwell J ...... "	7 36 8 19 11 52	1 4 4 12 5 26 6 17 7 47 9 45
4	Wolverton K 4 12, 4 25. arr.	7 42 8 22 9 11 56	1 18 4 16 5 33 6 21 7 51 9 49
54½	London (Euston)... arr.	9 4 19 59 11 40	9 11 36 10 ...9 11 22

Down.

Miles			Week Days only.
		mrn|mrn|mrn	aft|aft|aft|aft|aft|aft|aft
		S	S
—	412 London (Euston) ...dep.	6 45 7 35	12 15 3 6 ...5 10 7 15
—	Wolverton...... "	7 57 8 43 12 15 2 30 4 4 55 4 57 15	9 20 9 59
1	Great Linford...... "	8 3 8 46 12 18 3 34 4 65 4 87 22	9 23 10 2
2¼	Bradwell J ...... "	8 4 29 50 12 22 3 37 4 25 5 33 7 26	9 27 10 6
4	Newport Pagnell ......arr.	8 . 8 8 48 8 54 12 26 2 41 3 66 07 36	9 31 10 10

E Except Saturdays. J 1 mile to New Bradwell K Sta for Stony Stratford (2 miles)

S or S Saturdays only V 5 mins. later on Sats.

Wartime service on the branch in Bradshaw's Guide for 1942.

Bill Simpson Collection

A less familiar engine on the branch in May 1953. A Fairburn 2 cylinder 2-6-4 tank 42155. These were very much liked by the Bletchley crews as they described them as having a 'snappier' exhaust. 'We got ninety out of these on the 'up' locals to Euston', extolled Fred Bateman. The engine is not fitted for auto train working and as run-round. Less photographed is the unofficial practice of simply pushing the train back which was done often if the signalman was accommodating at Wolverton! A point to note for modellers of railway branch lines.

J House

batch of 12 tended to rotate between these lines with 41275, 41222 being regular incumbents. These were sometimes replaced on the branch with the less popular Fowler 2-6-2T 40043.

Rostering became more haphazard after the closure of Newport shed in 1954 when engines were sent up from Bletchley with their crews each morning. There would then be Stanier and Fairburn 2-6-4 tanks. Those seen on the branch include 42062, 42155, 42580, 42582, 42061, 42066 and 42669. Very often these engines were in an advanced pre-repair shop condition and were poor substitutes for the sprightly Ivatts. Engine

A less common visitor on the branch was the light 2-6-2 Standard Tank. In this view 84002 is simmering gently as her crew look on contemplatively on this late summer day of the 13 September, 1958 at Newport Pagnell station.

R K Blencowe

number 42669 had such worn valve gear that even when pulled up to mid-gear it still cut-off at 50%.

The worst steamer of all was 40043 it proved impossible to keep the pressure from falling below 80 lbs per square inch which brought the brakes on which had to be released by hand.

In the final years locum duty for the absent Ivatts went from aged and lame to the consummate strength of the new British Railways 2-6-4 ' Standard' Tank engines. For engines accustomed to working the smartly timed Bletchley – Euston locals of seven to eight coaches in the rush hour a spell on the branch was like going to a rest home. This sojourn is known to have been enjoyed by 80040, 80042, 80043, 80083, 84004 and 84002.

Not all engines were fitted with push-pull equipment so there had to be running round at each end. This applied in particular to a 2-6-4T.

The daily branch freight was worked by the tank engines but there were exceptions some noted took place in 1960. On the 8 July the freight was worked by 4F No. 44447 and on the 5 August the same duty by 4F 44364.

Driver Fred Baldwin on the left in charge of 80040 Standard 2-6-4T in 1957 at Newport Pagnell. Although the Standards were very powerful engines they were much heavier on water than the Stanier and Fairburn versions. Bletchley used them mainly on the Euston locals.

F G Cockman

Although Bletchley was working Diesel Multiple Units in 1956 there is no evidence that they were ever used on the Newport Pagnell branch. Nor any to suggest diesel usage on any passenger trains. The only recorded evidence is during the last days of the freight service after passenger closure in 1964 when The Derby Sulzer, later class 24 Type 2 diesels handled the daily coal train.

Turning to the more esoteric motive power there is information on the use of the experimental petro-electric railmotor in 1913 tested by the LNWR on the branch. Accessibility from Wolverton would make the line ideal for any impromptu testing. To the extremes, as the photographic evidence shows, even a streamlined pacific of the LMS 4-6-2 'Coronation' Class has travelled nearly a mile up the branch, probably to turn on the Wolverton triangle.

A remarkable picture to bear witness to such impressive power on a humble branch line. Engine 6220 'Coronation' of the 'Princess Coronation Class' being turned on the Wolverton Triangle. In preparation for the American tour in 1938, note fitting of headlamp. It is now generally known that 'Coronation' was not available and this engine was in truth 6229 'Duchess of Hamilton' this is a happy coincidence as the 'Duchess' seen here remains in service still. The two-lever frame being operated by the fireman was unlocked by Annett's Key.

Bill West Collection.

WOLVERTON (for STONY STRATFORD) AND NEWPORT PAGNELL.

WEEK DAYS ONLY.

Table **65**

								SO	SO	SX								SX			SO	SO	
London (Euston) .....dep.	...	...	685C	...	7 35	9 30	10 35	12 5	12 5	12 15	...	3 6	4 10	5 32	6 6	75X15	8A0	...	...	...	...	9 55	...
Wolverton (for Stony Stratford)...dep.	8 10	8 35	9 0	9 50	11 5	12 15	1 32	1 36	...	2 15	3 0	4 25	5 45	7 0	7 45	9 0	9 36	...	10 10	...	10 25	11 46	...
Bradwell	...	8 38	9 12	9 54	11 8	12 18	1 35	1 39	...	2 18	3 4	4 28	5 48	7 3	7 48	9 3	9 39	...	10 13	...	10 28	11 49	...
Great Linford	...	8 42	9 16	10 0	11 13	12 22	1 39	1 43	...	2 22	3 10	4 32	5 53	7 7	7 53	9 7	9 43	...	10 17	...	10 32	11 53	...
Newport Pagnell .....arr.	8 18	8 46	9 20	10 6	11 16	12 26	1 43	1 47	...	2 26	3 16	4 36	6 0	7 11	7 56	9 11	9 47	...	10 21	...	10 36	11 57	...
							SO			SO	SX	SO						SO	SX		SX	SO	SO
Newport Pagnell .....dep.	7 25	8 21	8 50	9 23	10 21	11 41	...	1 2	1 7	1 51	2 31	3 47	5 22	6 6	6 23	7 19	8 30	9 14	9 51	10 4	11 22	...	...
Great Linford	7 27	8 23	8 52	9 25	10 23	11 43	...	1 6	1 9	1 53	2 33	3 49	5 24	6 8	6 27	7 21	8 32	9 16	9 53	10 6	11 24	...	...
Bradwell	7 33	8 28	8 57	9 30	10 28	11 48	...	1 12	1 14	1 58	2 38	3 54	5 29	6 13	6 32	7 26	8 37	9 21	9 58	10 11	11 29	...	...
Wolverton (for Stony Stratford) arr.	7 39	8 32	9 1	9 34	10 32	11 52	...	1 18	1 18	2 2	2 42	3 58	5 33	6 17	6 36	7 30	8 41	9 25	10 2	10 15	11 33	...	...
London (Euston) .....arr.	9 34	...	10 15	11 20	12a 0	...	...	2 37	2 41	...	4 2	5637	75X5	7 50	8 42	...	10g40	11 39	...	...	...	...	...

A—On Sats. departs London (Eus.) 7.15 p.m.

a—On Sats. arrives London (Eus.) 12.10 p.m.

B—On Saturdays departs London (Euston) 7.0 a.m.

b—Arrives London (Eus.) 6.30 p.m. on Sats.

d—Stops to set down only.

f—On Saturdays arrive London (Euston) 4.10 p.m.

g—On Saturdays arrive London (Euston) 11.9 p.m.

SO—Saturdays only.

SX—Saturdays excepted.

Timetable of trains on the branch in 1939 with connections for London Euston. With a weekday service of some fourteen trains in both directions this must represent the high point of the branch line service. The last train of that day on Saturday, the 11.24 connecting with the 9.55 from Euston was very popular with theatregoers.

Bradshaws Guide

The Wolverton to Newport Pagnell branch did not change from steam to diesel for passenger trains. It just about managed to witness this replacement motive power in the shape of Sulzer Class 24 Bo Bo's from 1966 to 1967 on the daily goods. This was mainly coal and scrap iron for Goodmans. Bletchley lost steam in 1966 and D5034 is a loco that carried out this daily trip.

Brian Sessions

Propelling vehicles on running lines outside station limits—Rule 149—continued.

From	To	Line.	Wagons or other vehicles (limited to No. in figures where shown—exclusive of brake van) which may be propelled.
Wolverton No. 2	Facing points to triangle on Newport Pagnell Branch	Single	Coaching stock and freight wagons without brake van.
Facing points to triangle on Newport Pagnell branch	Wolverton No. 2	Single	,, ,, ,,
Bradwell	,, No. 2	Single	Freight wagons without brake van.
Newport Pagnell	,, No. 2	Single	2 milk vans. In clear weather only.

In the General Appendix to the Working Time Tables Rule 149 Refers to the propelling of vehicles on running lines outside station limits.

Another interesting aside that looked like it would become a serious possibility was the LNWR plans to electrify the line with the same system as the Lancashire & Yorkshire installation between Liverpool and Southport. This was announced in May 1904. It appears that this prospect did not meet with enthusiasm from the newly promoted Chief Mechanical Engineer George Whale and went no further. An interesting might-have-been.

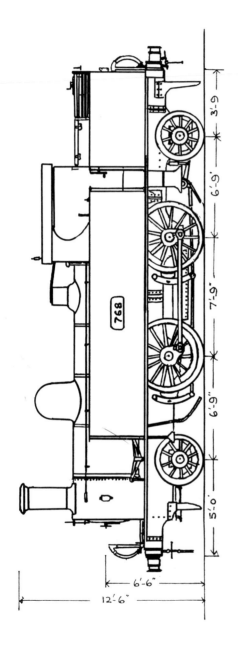

The passenger services of the line were operated often in LNWR days by the 4ft 6in and 5ft 6in 2-4-2 tanks locally known as 'Chopper Tanks'.

Drawing by Fred Bateman

4mm to 1 foot scale

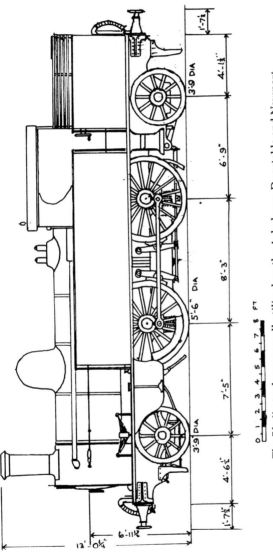

The 5ft 6in tanks were well utilised on the Aylesbury, Dunstable and Newport Pagnell branches for light passenger work and lasted into the early 1950's.

Drawing by Fred Bateman

4mm to 1 foot scale

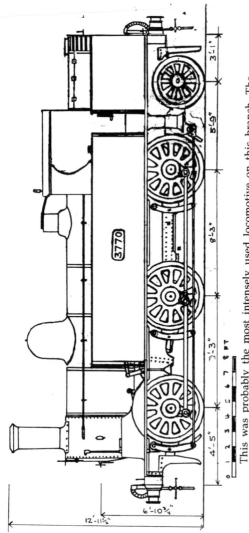

This was probably the most intensely used locomotive on this branch. The LNWR built 300 from 1881 onwards, a development of the 0-6-0 Coal Engine. Their success on passenger work led to the LMS fitting them with vacuum control apparatus for push-pull working. Happily one of them is amongst the few LNWR engines to survive into preservation.

Drawing by Fred Bateman

4mm to 1 foot scale

94

No. 46 With driver in coach driving position the 12.50 (SO) departs from Newport Pagnell with 41222 propelling on the 22 August, 1964. Apparently against the platform starting signal.

A Swain.

CHAPTER FIVE

Coaches in use on the Branch

For the following information I am indebted to the research work of Richard Casserley.

Although the LNWR turned to six-wheel stock about 1871, quite a number of four wheel surburban sets were built between 1890 and 1900, many of these coaches lasting until 1955-6 Six-wheel stock was also in service on the Bletchley branches into the 1930's. Set No. 1. had the same vehicles from September 1909 until June 1925 and probably until 1930. These were LNWR Nos 7575,3001,1876,6864 (1876 was added to the set in

A valuable photograph of a train in the full LNWR period having just left Bradwell with a train for Wolverton. The 2-4-2 tank, horse box and three six-wheel coaches in carmine lake and ermine white livery typifies a very long period in the line's history. The train is obviously running pre-1920 when the push- pull trains were introduced.

Wolverton Archeological Society.

about 1912. Coaches 7575 and 6864 were 30 ft 1 in brake thirds, 3001 a 28 ft four-wheeled composite of 1894, whilst 1876 was 30 ft 1 in.

The workmen's set withdrawn from the Newport Pagnell branch in November 1959 included two of the oldest coaches of the LNWR still in service. Two of them had the cove roof abandoned in 1907! These were thirds 13815 and 13797 and a brake third 22414. The first two dated from 1908 whilst the latter dated from 1906. Reason for withdrawal at that time was the result of damage due to an accident at Newport Pagnell on 19 September 1959.

Coaches of the morning and evening Wolverton workmens train in the goods yard siding at Newport Pagnell in 1958. Closest to the camera is an LNWR 50 ft non-corridor brake. The coaches were in this position on Saturday 21 September 1959 when the 7.48 am ex- Wolverton overshot the platform and the Ivatt Tank ran into the LNWR coach hastening its departure to the scrap yard. For the remaining years the train was composed of ex-LMS stock.

HMRS

Early coach use on the branch was four-wheelers of pre- 1871 origin which lasted until May 1904. These were gas lit with flat flame burners. The four-wheelers were then replaced by 30 ft 6 in six-wheelers of 1871-7 which were in turn withdrawn between 1907-11.

Coach bodies that appeared on the platform were first of all a North London Railway third 1101 which was sent to serve as an office in August 1921. This was followed about 1930 with a 30 ft 1 in parcels sorting van.

Another dedicated branch set from January 1919 until January 1927 were four LNWR six-wheel vehicles Nos 6871,2615,340,6535. these were all 30 ft vehicles, 2615 being the composite.

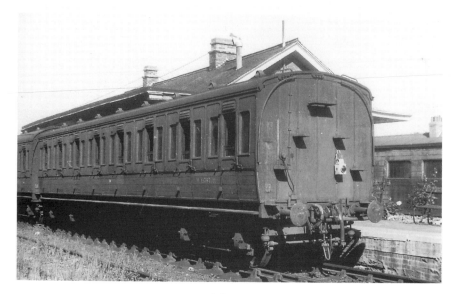

(a)

(b)

(c)

After an accident in 1959 involving a train overunning the platform and hitting the ex-LNWR workmen's coaches they were withdrawn from service in November. They were replaced with newly painted non-corridor stock. Thoughtfully the writer and photographer, the late H C Casserley did a photo survey of the set before the accident in April of that year. His photographs are accompanied with his notes:

(a) LNWR 50'x 9'third built Wolverton 1906. A second/third composite for Birmingham District Sets. 83 built between 1903-7, extinct by 1959, no M13797 was badly damaged, buffer beam knocked away, two compartments demolished and the frame buckled by the impact.

(b) LNWR 50'x 9'third built Wolverton 1908, Birmingham District Sets, 27 built 1907-9 no M13815.

(c) LNWR 50' x 9' third built Wolverton 1906. Also 1093 for Birmingham District Sets 16. 86 built 1903-7 extinct by 1959 no M22414.

H C Casserley

99

A splendid photographic study of No.41289 and train waiting at Newport Pagnell in the 1960's. It is obviously high summer, if this were a colour photograph it would very likely be dominated by the colours of the station garden in the foreground.
Bill Turner.

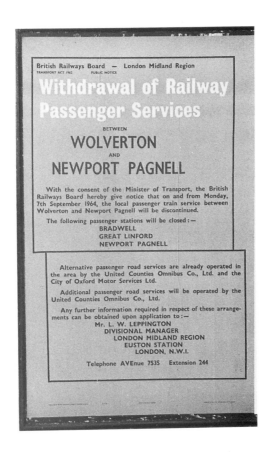

CHAPTER SIX

End of the Line

After the Second World War most people's dreams were centred on having a modern clean labour saving house and travelling about in their own car.

After the First World War as a result of wartime service many working people had the ability to drive. In the Second World War the same occurred but more so as it was the first truly mechanised war in history. Road haulage had been developing throughout the thirties and continued to do so in the fifties especially after the removal of petrol restrictions in 1954.

Engine 41222 just arrived with the 8.33am from Wolverton to a bright sunny morning in August 1964.

Peter Baughan

The railways had now to come to terms with the prospect of a car owning democracy and organised transport, undertakings like British Road Services. The answer had been the British Transport Commission set up by Government in 1948. The early years of the BTC are absorbing reading in themselves but beyond the scope of this book. Sufficient to say that the altruistic ideal born of the Labour Government was to have an integrated transport system. A prospect with much to commend it and with which few would fault. However, succeeding governments and transport ministers did not believe that this was a realistic possibility. The new dynamics of road communication were being harnessed to the nineteenth century concept of railways and canals, the BTC therefore was wound up in 1962. In its place came the regional railway boards, London

DOWN

Mileage (M C): WOLVERTON 0 0 · Bradwell 1 14 · Great Linford 2 67 · NEWPORT PAGNELL 4 1

Service	Days	WOLVERTON (dep)	Bradwell	Great Linford	NEWPORT PAGNELL (arr)
Rail Motor		am 7 48	…	…	7 56
Rail		am 8 35	8 39	8 43	8 46
Mixed		am 10 0	10 4	10 8	10 11
Rail Motor	SO	PM 12 25	12 29	12 33	12 36
Rail	SO	PM 1 33	1 37	1 41	1 44
Mixed		PM 2 40	2 44	2 48	2 51
Rail		PM 4 50	4 54	4 58	5 1
Rail Motor	SX	PM 5 43	5 47	5b52	5 55
Rail Motor	SO	PM 5 43	5 47	5b52	5 55
Rail Motor	SX	PM 8 0	8 4	8 8	8 11
Rail Motor	SX	PM 9 0	9 4	9 8	9 11
Rail Motor	SO	PM 9 5	…	9 13	9 16
Rail Motor	SO	PM 9 46	9N50	9 54	9 57
Rail Motor	SX	PM 9 53	9N57	10 1	10 4
Rail Motor	SO	PM 10 35	10N39	10 43	10 46

N Bradwell tickets to be collected at Wolverton.

NEWPORT PAGNELL TO WOLVERTON

WEEKDAYS

UP

Mileage (M C): NEWPORT PAGNELL 0 0 · Great Linford 1 14 · Bradwell 2 67 · WOLVERTON 4 1

Service	Days	NEWPORT PAGNELL (dep)	Great Linford	Bradwell	WOLVERTON (arr)
Rail Motor (Not advertised)		am 6 15	6 19	…	6 25
Rail Motor		am 7 15	7 18	7b24	7 29
Rail Motor		am 8 3	8 6	8 11	8 14
Rail Motor		am 8 52	8b56	9 1	9 4
Rail	SO	am 11 40	11 43	11 48	11 51
Rail Motor	SO	PM 1 50	1 53	1 58	2 1
Rail Motor		PM 4 5	4 8	4 13	4 16
Mixed		PM 5 17	5 20	5 25	5 28
Rail		PM 6 3	6 6	6 11	6 14
Rail Motor		PM 8 35	8 38	8 43	8 46
Rail Motor	SX	PM 9 20	9 23	9 28	9 31
Rail Motor	SO	PM 9 25	…	9 33	9 36
Rail Motor	SO	PM 10 0	10 3	10 8	10 11

Working timetable for 1953.

Bill Simpson Collection

In the sunlight of a Saturday afternoon 41222 arrives at Newport Pagnell with the 12.25 from Wolverton. End of the working week, the workmen's coaches are placed in the silent goods yard until Monday morning. It is the 22 of August, 1964 and the branch knows that this is the last summer, in four weeks it will close.

A Swain

Midland Region being responsible for the west coast main line and of course Wolverton and the Newport Pagnell Branch.

After intense lobbying from road users the much vaunted system of new auto-age specially designed motorways, was brought into being with the opening of the M1 from London to Birmingham in November 1959. From now on the railways would be fighting a retreating battle on every front.

The £1240 million modernization scheme of 1955 had foretold the end of the steam locomotive in definite terms. This could be no surprise, the large pre-grouping companies had before 1914 been experimenting with electric power. The Southern Railway had electrified 748 track miles by 1930 and was continuing to advance this power as much as possible until World War Two affected its progress. The London Midland & Scottish Railway were more than pleased with their fleet of diesel shunters and continued experiments with passenger prototypes. Indeed part of the remit of the BTC was to instigate a new traction policy. The last days of the steam locomotive were inextricably linked with the national pride, a machine that changed the world had come out of British workshops. diesels were foreign in invention and concept.

A much greater blow to follow this was announced in the report compiled for the Ministry of Transport by Dr Richard Beeching in his 'Reshaping of British Railways' in 1963. To remove from the system altogether some 6,000 miles of track and therefore railway service to many communities. There is much else in the report, some things good, like

WOLVERTON TO NEWPORT PAGNELL. WEEKDAYS A215

DOWN

Mileage M	C			B (Rail Motor)	B (Rail Motor)	B (Mixed)	B (Rail Motor)	B (Mixed)	B (Mixed)	B (Rail Motor)	B (Rail Motor)	B (Rail Motor)	B	B (Rail Motor)
							SO	SO	SX	SO	SX	SO	SX	SO
				am	am	am	PM	PM	PM	PM	PM	PM	PM	PM
0	0	WOLVERTON dep	1	7 48	8 35	10 0	12 25	1 33	2 40	2 45	4 37	4 50	5 43	5 43
1	8	Bradwell	2	7 52	8 39	10 4	12 29	1 37	2 44	2 49	4 41	4 54	5b52	5b52
2	60	Great Linford	3	7 56	8 43	10 8	12 33	1 41	2 48	2 53	4 45	4 58	5 55	5 55
3	76	NEWPORT PAGNELL arr	4	7 59	8 46	10 11	12 36	1 44	2 51	2 56	4 48	5 1	5 55	5 55

NEWPORT PAGNELL TO WOLVERTON WEEKDAYS

UP

Mileage M	C			B (Rail Motor)	B (Rail Motor)	B (Rail Motor)	B (Rail Motor)	B (Rail Motor)	B (Rail Motor)	B (Rail Motor)	B (Rail Motor)	B (Mixed)
					SO	SX		SO		SO		
				am	am	am	am	am	PM	PM	PM	PM	PM
0	0	NEWPORT PAGNELL dep	1	7 15	8 3	8 15	8 49	11 40	1 0	1 50	4 0	5 17	6 3
1	16	Great Linford	2	7 18	8 6	8 18	8 52	11 43	1 3	1 53	4 3	5 20	6 6
2	68	Bradwell	3	7b24	8 11	8 23	8 57	11 48	1 8	1 58	4 8	5 25	6 11
3	76	WOLVERTON arr	4	7 29	8 14	8 26	9 0	11 51	1 11	2 1	4 11	5 28	6 14

Timetable for June 1961. The closure of the Newport Pagnell steam shed in 1954 had a depressing affect on the branch. For this effectively ended the evening service. The last train left Newport at 6.03 pm!

British Railways

liner trains (freightliner) but the overall effect of it was to give the railways for the first time a secondary role as the prime mover of the inland transport system.

What all of this preamble leads to is that the Newport Pagnell branch is listed for closure in the report and Wolverton works was relegated to a repair centre. The paternal association between company and employees was breaking up. Remaining employees of Wolverton Works would have to find their own means of getting there, or seek employment elsewhere. Two stations that ran regular workmen's trains were Castlethorpe and Roade, they were also listed for closure. What Sir Peter Parker came to refer to as 'The crumbling edge of the service' thirty years later first became noticeable on the Newport Pagnell branch in the headline front page of 'The Wolverton Express' on 4 December 1953. This reported on a meeting of the Newport Pagnell Urban District Council where it had been discovered that the BTC were planning to remove passenger trains on the branch after 7 pm. In detail this meant the cancellation of the 8.35 pm, 9.20 pm 10 pm, and late Saturday night trains from Newport Pagnell to Wolverton. Grave suspicions were raised, no doubt some locals would be mindful that the Cheddington—Aylesbury service had ceased its passenger trains that year and it little needs to be emphasized what impression it makes on the public when trains start to be removed from the timetable.

Whatever was felt about the alterations it did not effect them being implemented as by 1957 the last train from Newport Pagnell daily was the 6.03 pm, designated 'Mixed'.

The first notice of withdrawal of total service by the LMR appears on Monday 4 November 1963. After objection the deadline was withdrawn pending an enquiry and consideration by the TUCC.*

The first TUCC hearing took place on Tuesday 7 January, 1964 at Wolverton College of Further Education.

Mr Reynolds, Divisional Manager from British Railways Board said that replacement of the service by buses would require five 60 seat double decker and a subsidy of £6,000. Doubtless trying to bait the bus operators with the carrot of full buses plus subsidy. In effect admitting that a lot of people use the train. Later in the meeting he tries to argue the other way by saying that the figures are misleading, only one or two people travel on some trains.

* The Transport Users' Consultative Committee.

He stated further that British Railways had already approached United Counties Bus Services who wanted a subsidy of £10,000 per annum, £3,000 being attributable to the Castlethorpe service. The objectors quickly pointed out that the deficit claim by the Railways Board for Castlethorpe station was £1,400 per annum.

Mr Arthur Leary, representing Wolverton Carriage Works employees, said that 93 men travelled to Newport Pagnell from outlying villages to catch the train.

Mr J B Harwood, Clerk to the Wolverton Urban District Council said that there were 80 passengers who were not railway employees who preferred to travel by train. Either because the bus stop was further away or because the buses ran at inconvenient times. Also some remarked that they suffered from travel sickness, not affected by train travel.

In conclusion Mr F A Hall, Clerk to the Newport Pagnell Urban District Council asked for an adjournment as details of additional bus services had been put in at the last moment.

Wolverton station on 5 September 1964 a four coach train for regular engine Ivatt 2-6-2 tank 41222. Possibly to cater for all that would wish to ride the 'Newport Nobby' for the last time, as this was the last day of the passenger service.

K C H Fairey.

Guard Sam Wallis hands a floral wreath to the train crew of Ivatt 2-6-2T on the 5 September 1964 on the final train.

K C H Fairey.

The final Saturday trains with crowds of farewell wishers. The coach body behind them is a 30 ft 1 inch Parcels Sorting Van that appears to have replaced the London Railway vehicles as a store.

L Hanson

The final day of the service was overlayed with some sardonic humour, crowds and bunting did, at least show that 'Newport Nobby' was genuinely regarded with some affection and some impromptu 'Mrs Mops' ensured that she went into history cleanly.

Ray Bailey.

Impersonating Dr Beeching (Ralph Mazzone) sportingly accepts an expression from the people of Newport Pagnell intended for the notorious Doctor, a fire bucket of cold water. The last 'Newport Nobby' waits to leave.

Dr M Chappell

Bustle on the final day of the passenger service, Saturday, 5 September, 1964. The Ivatt engine 41222 arrived on the branch in 1953 and remained to haul this, the 6.01 pm train to its journey's end. During the day the normal two coaches sufficed, nos M17933M and M24415M. However for the 16.55 from Wolverton so many farewell takers and enthusiasts had gathered that the workmen's coaches had to pressed into service. A result of need and a fitting end, for all its 97 years the workmen had made it their own branch. The driver of the last train was a Bill Faulkner.

L Hanson

Published in the *Railway Observer* in March 1964 was a contribution from a traveller on the 2.45 pm train on the 1 February 1964. Fifty people used the train with children, prams and bicycles also on board. This gives an indication of usage outside the daily rote of the workmen's trains.

Whatever reasoned argument was expressed behind the scenes the timescale of 1964 suggests that the Ministry were determined on closure within the year come whatever. The bus alternative proposals were finally proclaimed in the local press with the following list.

The end of the line and the start of another. The buffer stops seen here should in fact have been the extended railway to Olney, that was never completed. The rails seen leading from it to the camera are those of the later Tramway that also never reached its destination. Background right the station, on the left, Coales's Mill.

Ray Bailey.

As a justification of closure the Minister made great accord to the availability of alternative buses. The service provided by United Counties Omnibus Company Ltd.,

No.130 & 132	Stony Stratford – Wolverton – Bradwell - Newport Pagnell – Bedford.
No.134	Stony Stratford – Wolverton – Great Linford - Newport Pagnell – North Crawley.
No.387	Stony Stratford – Wolverton – Bradwell - Bletchley.
No.391	Stony Stratford – Wolverton – Bradwell.
No.392	Stony Stratford – Wolverton – Bradwell.

A service provided jointly with UCC and the City of Oxford.

No.131	Oxford – Buckingham – Wolverton – Bradwell - Newport Pagnell – Bedford.

Actual day of closure of Newport Pagnell Railway branch was Monday 7 September, 1964. Goods stations of Newport Pagnell, Bradwell to close in December 1964.

This meant that the summer of 1964 was the last for the branch passengers. Three hundred railwaymen would complete their holidays with the knowledge that they had to find a new way of going to work. Seventy schoolchildren would have to have different arrangements made for them by their parents, quite an upheaval.

An eye witness describes the branch in August 1964, 'Regular Engine 41222 is handling the passenger trains which do not appear to be quite so plentifully booked as may be supposed.' To be fair this is after all the height of the holiday season. 'The dilapidated state of the station tends to discourage use, no one wants to be reminded of the eventual decay of all things. Engine 42106 appears to be handling the daily goods trains from Wolverton coming out and getting back within the hour. The same engine handles the morning and evening workmen's train.'

It is worth mentioning that even at this stage the goods trains could be handling as many as sixty wagons in a train on the branch. If they were fully loaded it would require all the braking exertions of even a Stanier tank on 1 in 80! That may well have been a contributing factor in the rostering of 0-6-0 4F engines on the job.

The siding to Coales, formerly Hives that left the station and crossing the road at Newport Pagnell was disconnected by the railway in the late 1950's.

The two-pronged siding at Bradwell was now used by a scrap dealer and was loaded with wagons of scrap. The extreme curve on this siding leads to the frequent fouling of the Ivatt tank bogies which lifted and dropped over the side. It happened so regularly that the crews became quite adept at wedging and re-railing the wheels.

As photographs show, the people of Newport Pagnell were not going to let the local affectionately regarded train cease with a whimper.

The last train ran on Saturday 6 September, 1964. It appears that the 'Wake' like celebrations had the echo of those long ago jubilant days when the railway opened to a very different Newport Pagnell. The local youth club registered their gratitude by passing out cigars to the driver and fireman of the last train. Remembering all those Christmases when Santa Claus forsook his traditional reindeer and came on the train to hand out presents at their Annual Bazaar.

'Newport Nobby' steamed in at 5.58 pm when immediately two men dressed as Mrs Mop cleaners gave the train a brisk clean with buckets of water, so that the very last journey should be more presentable on arrival at Wolverton.

A rather game 'Dr. Beeching' (Ralph Mazzone) received the contents of one bucket of water over his bowler-hatted head. This was greatly appreciated by a considerable crowd that had gathered on the platform.

It seems that the train was waved and cheered away with all the regret of a departing companion as depicted in the Ealing film *The Titfield Thunderbolt* — but this train was not to return. From those final heady moments the story was of gradual winding down.

CHAPTER SEVEN

Silent Stations

From the September of passenger closure up until the following June there was a single weekday goods remaining on the working timetable, this left Wolverton at 10.30 m and arrived at Newport Pagnell 11.00 m. It had forty minutes to shunt whatever was required and leave by 11.40 m to be back at Wolverton by 12.10 m. Anything from or to Bradwell Siding was dealt with on the journey.

By October of 1965 type 2, believed to be class 24 diesels were working this train. During the same period Wolverton No. 2 and No. 1 signalboxes were demoted to shunting frames as the new power box at Bletchley came into action and the Wolverton starting signal on the branch was removed.

In December it was reported that the branch line had been taken out of use and the line severed between Wolverton north shunting frame and triangle ground frame. The triangle ground frame had been taken out of use as it was clipped spiked and padlocked for the direction only of Wolverton South GF.

The last working train on the branch consisted mainly of coal deliveries which would soon be subject to alterations to a grander scheme.

Newport Pagnell shortly before closure, the poster enthusiastically proclaims the West Coast main line electrics of the sixties, but the silent station, that now knows its fate, is filled with sunlight and melancholy.

Lens of Sutton

This was largely speaking as a result of the introduction of block train working in the Beeching Plan. New trains would bring the coal to central depots in 500 ton loads in 21 ton hopper wagons. Such a depot was announced for Wolverton to provide a catchment area for Newport Pagnell, Olney, Castlethorpe, Woburn Sands, Fenny Stratford, Bletchley, Swanbourne, Winslow and Buckingham, all stations that were closed or proposed for closure with the exception of Wolverton and Bletchley. The depot for Wolverton proposed early in 1966 will have on site 5,000 tons at any one time and be capable of holding 80,000, obviously a contingency for stockpiling. Coal merchants will be expected to attend the depot for their loadings.

The branch was finally severed on 31 December 1966 to make way for the new coal depot. The water tower at Bradwell had been demolished in August. The buildings of both intermediate stations were demolished in the summer of 1967 and track was removed.

Freight services on the branch were officially closed on the 22 May 1967. These had been accessed by the south curve only. By Monday 5 August 1968 the track and signals at Newport Pagnell and from there to Bradwell had been removed. A buffer stop had been erected at the end of the remaining track, about 50 yards west of the road bridge at Bradwell.

The coal concentration depot was closed after its short life on 3 July 1972 and its facilities were adapted to deal with roadstone for the new town of Milton Keynes. What remained of the branch was used as an extended 'elbow' siding until 1973 when it was replaced with a proper siding adjacent to the 'up' slow line.

Whatever may be said about 28 years or so since the branch closed one thing is significant and that is the fact that a vast majority of the population have had to come to terms with this kind of change.

Apart from the effect of Wars the concept of change in the past has been of gradual assimilation. Not so the modern world where processes are contracted from years to months and days.

Indigenous local services like 'Newport Nobby' and the 'Dunstable Dasher' that would continue their daily rote of journeys as a background to town and village life past church fetes and cricket matches retaining a regularity that underlined that sense of permanence. They would be there the next year and the next, carrying workers, shoppers, schoolchildren, the odd days outing, coping with winter snow or slowing down for a flock of sheep. Always taking and bringing local produce and people through cheer and tragedy. Even the staff of the line would be local townspeople.

Such local feeling and ties to the Branch line that are left, is at best tentative. The Beeching era took away the certainties of such times and the bland diesels are so much like road vehicles.

Modern trains are clean and efficient and do their job well. However, they are not so personalized as in the days of branch line steam, their corporate colours emphasize them as part of a corporate system.

The loss of the branch line railway and the decline of public transport since the War has greater social consequences than the removal of anachronisms. People travelling together came to know each other better, they nourished the community spirit, the common purpose and the common destination, the workmen's trains, the school trains, shopping trips etc., The modern routine of lone journeys by car to and from work and at home closed in with television viewing, is far less sociable.

When the railway opened in the Newport Pagnell district in 1838 the road system fell into decline. One hundred and twenty-one years later it

After the end of the passenger service the overgrown and weedy desolation. Of interest are the rails leading off on the right that originally crossed the road and entered Hives Corn Mill in 1876.

Ray Bailey.

A largely unphotographed view from the end of the goods yard.

Ray Bailey

Now derelict, the large goods shed at Newport Pagnell.

Ray Bailey.

The distant and derelict goods shed to which engines must not pass. Extended beyond the station, built on land intended for the Olney extension, it now has only demolition in prospect, in the late sixties.

Ray Bailey

The former LNWR yard crane at Newport Pagnell.

Ray Bailey.

A wagon turntable alongside the goods shed at Newport Pagnell. Commonly used with men and horse shunting throughout the nineteenth century. This one gave access to Price's Corn Mill siding which emphasizes the laborious pace of working it.

Ray Bailey.

119

WEEKDAYS   WOLVERTON AND NEWPORT PAGNELL

DOWN

Mileage M	C				K (282)	K (282)		K (281)
					SX Q am	am		SX PM
0	0	WOLVERTON	.. dep	1	6 45	11 55	..	1 40
1	8	Bradwell	.... arr	2	......	12 0	......	1 45
			.... .. dep	3	....	12 30	..	1 53
3	76	NEWPORT PAGNELL	.... arr	4	6 56	12 40	......	2 5

Also conveys motor set

UP

Mileage M	C			K (282)	K (281)	
				SX Q am	SX PM	
0	0	NEWPORT.. .. .. .. PAGNELL	1	11 30	2 15	..
3	76	WOLVERTON	2	11 40	2 25	......

Working timetable for the mid-fifties daily freight, note the 6.45 am from Wolverton conveys Motor Set.

Bill Simpson Collection

got its revenge when the first trunk route motorway was opened between London and Birmingham — M1. The railway enhanced the commerce and prosperity of the nation improving the standard of living of all. The appetite of motorways hungers by what it feeds on, unchecked they may well devour all the good they have done in a way that railways never did.

Thanks to local authorities like the Milton Keynes Development Association it is possible to conclude this branch line history on a happier note. So many lines once belonging to the national concern have been sold off and their access lost to the public. In view of the congestion and danger of the modern roads this is doubly regrettable as a very attractive and safe alternative to modern roads covering thousands of miles have been lost. Exceptions to this loss are the footpath and cycleways like the Cromford and High Peak Trail, Tissington Trail which have proved the point. The Newport Pagnell branch is I am glad to say one of those exceptions. It is still possible to walk or cycle between Wolverton and Newport Pagnell in safety and in attractive surroundings. Ideal for children learning to ride bicycles and for the young pony rider, it has an enclosed equestrian way as well. If we must lose the railway I can think of no better alternative, the line still goes on serving the community even without its rails! The platforms of Bradwell and Great Linford remain to rest and picnic and the entire route is illuminated. Perhaps on some mid-summers eve through the birdsong of gladed confines the ghostly whistle of 'Newport Nobby' calls back along that pathway.

February 9, 1968

DEATH OF A RAILWAY

Workmen rip up 'Nobby's' 4-mile track

There's no doubt about it. Newport Pagnell's branch railway line is dead !

There can be no last minute reprieve, no revival to meet the needs of the new city of Milton Keynes, no preservation as a museum piece for railway enthusiasts or film companies.

A look at this picture taken this week at New Bradwell shows why.

Gone are the station buildings and up come the sleepers and iron rails that carried successive Newport "Nobbys" on the four-mile, 11-minute journey from Wolverton to Newport Pagnell.

The "iron road" is now no more than a cinder track carrying the most unusual traffic of motor lorries collecting the up-ended sleepers.

It was in September, 1964, that the branch line was closed to passenger traffic despite a public outcry and tremendous opposition at a local inquiry.

The railway that had in its time carried millions of workmen, schoolchildren and holidaymakers was relegated to an infrequent service for goods traffic.

Understandably this traffic became less and the service

So the branch line died just over a hundred years after Newport Pagnell's church bells rang out to greet the ceremonial opening for passenger traffic on September 2, 1867.

Five years earlier, on June 16, 1863, the bells had rung out to mark the passing of the Newport Pagnell Railway Act through the committee stage in the House of Commons, despite opposition from the Grand Junction Canal Company.

The estimated cost of building the line was £45,000 with a five years' completion time. On September 30, 1865, the first engine ran from Wolverton to Newport haul.

The railway brought many benefits to traders and to people wishing to travel quickly to other parts of the country. It was also easier for people to get to Newport and the famous Newport Pagnell Steeplechases were revived.

Within eight years the company amalgamated with the old LNWR and by 1904 there were even suggestions of electrification.

In 1911 second class carriages and fares were withdrawn and in 1955 the line lost its "Nobby" which had been housed in a corrugated iron engine shed a little way out of the station.

The Wolverton Express publicize the dismantling of a very popular railway, the sign is from the Bradwell siding.

Wolverton Express

These are the details of the working timetable from the 7 September 1964 (Monday after closure) to the 13 June 1965. This timetable for the single goods working of mainly coal and scrap iron was the only diesel rostering on the branch. Sulzer Class 24 Bo Bo's of Bletchley new diesel depot took over when the steam shed closed in 1966. It continued until the 22 of May 1967 when, only a few months short of its Centenary the line closed completely.

Saturdays Excepted

		am			am
Wolverton		10.30	Newport Pagnell		11.40
Bradwell	arr	10.35			
	dep	10.45			pm
Newport Pagnell		11.00	Wolverton		12.10

CHAPTER EIGHT

Epilogue

The following account is written by and from the experiences of Mr F G Cockman, he had the good fortune to experience driving on the branch. As a railway author, amongst his many works are the wonderful little books *Discovering Lost Railways* and *Discovering Preserved Railways*. The following account is vividly detailed as a man accustomed to writing would communicate. It takes the interesting position of the enlightened novice having a go.

'Driving on the Newport Pagnell Branch I first became acquainted with this interesting branch line in the early 1950's. Until May 1954 Newport had its own shed with accommodation for one engine. The train services were provide by two crews, namely – Fred Baldwin, driver and his fireman Ronnie (whose surname I never knew), and the other driver Cyril Holman and his mate Ken Langly. They were extremely competent at their job and very friendly, so that if you expressed and intelligent interest in their engine, you soon found yourself on the footplate.

It was only a matter of time before you were taught how to fire and drive, of course under their supervision. The branch saw a good variety of tank engines, but not tender engines, hardly needed for four miles.

I remember very well Ivatt 2-6-2T 41222 which stayed on the branch for some years. I usually travelled on the 13.00 Newport Pagnell to Wolverton

Action! Ramsbottom 0-6-0 of Wolverton Works Traction Dept. achieves the role of passenger locomotive for some apparently patriotic moment during a film being shot possibly sometime in the nineteen fifties at Newport Pagnell station. The poster on the left extols London Midland fast freight with a picture of a Stanier Black Five, preceding the days of dynamic posters claiming the service by diesel and electric. The 'Station Master's Office' sign has been produced by the film company.

Dr M Chappell

and my job, on arriving at the station was to make up the fire with a few shovels and put on the injector after checking the water level in the boiler. The injectors on the 2-6-2T were a delight and they sang into action immediately. This was in contrast to the Black 5 4-6-0 which often had tricky injectors.

On receiving the 'right away' from the porter one gave a glance at the starting signal which was always 'off' and the engine then made light of its two coach load, with the regulator on first valve cut-off gradually reduced from 30% to 20%. The instructions I was given was to shut off steam at the timber crossings, about 100 yards from Great Linford station and to pull up precisely at the short platform. I must say that I found the vacuum brake most responsive and I never had any difficulty in stopping at the right spot.

The next section was the hardest, the engine having to climb the gradient of 1 in 80 up to the iron bridge (over the Grand Union Canal). You looked out from the cemetery where you shut off steam just right to stop gently in Bradwell station. The next part was easy as you started on a slight down grade and then steamed slowly round the triangle which led to Wolverton station. Here the injector was put on again to 'keep her quiet' until the return to Newport at 14.45.

I remember once on the return journey preparing to open the regulator on receiving the 'right away' from the porter, having my arm sharply jolted away from the control. 'Look at the signal!' said Cyril, sure enough, the arm was still at danger. It was soon pulled off but I never forgot the lesson.

You took the train gently round the triangle then down and up to Bradwell, shutting of power as you crossed over a culvert. At Bradwell you had to be sure to keep about twelve inches of vacuum to prevent the train moving back as the passengers were boarding the train. Starting off you opened the regulator at the same time creating 21 inches of vacuum. Then there was the slight rise to iron bridge, where you closed the regulator and ran down the 1 in 80 to Great Linford. The final part was on a slight down grade, steam being shut off at the Newport Pagnell fixed distant, so into the station. This down grade could be tricky on a wet day, because if you were clumsy with the brake the engine wheels would pick up and you slid a little too far down the platform with a feeling of gratitude that the buffers were still 100 yards further on. This was a delightful engine to drive.

Of course not all not all engines were like 41222. I remember one brute

58887, a Webb 'Coal Tank'. This no doubt had been an excellent machine when built in 1882, but now considerably the worse for wear. For example the regulator was not steam tight so the locomotive had to stand in Newport station with the brakes (vacuum and hand) hard on, in mid- gear and the cylinder cocks open. So it was always enveloped in a cloud of steam, you knew, from a distance, if this engine had been rostered for the train.

A glance at the water gauge showed that the boiler was in a filthy condition, all ready to prime. On receiving the signal to start you carefully set the cut-off at 40% where it stayed and the regulator was opened half way. The cylinder cocks were of course shut. Any attempt to give more steam would result in a bad attack of priming with water coming out of the chimney, but we did get to Wolverton.

Another unattractive feature was the vacuum brake, instead of the modern LMS control you had Webb's flap valve. The vacuum pipe was placed on the left hand side of the cab and was equipped with a flap. This you raised to apply the brakes and the air would rush in; if you found that you were slowing down too soon, you dropped the flap and the brakes eventually came off. But it was a tricky business stopping at the right place in the station platforms.

We also had a curiosity in no 40043, a Fowler 2-6-2T. These had done very well on the Moorgate to Barking services when introduced in 1930, but by 1953 with six years of war neglect it was a poor tool. To make matters worse I found that the engine's bunker was full of what looked like pieces of stone and some coal dust. Of course the engine would not burn this stuff but we did manage to make Great Linford. However the climb up to the iron bridge was asking too much and we stopped in Bradwell with 80lbs on the clock and the brakes leaking on. There was nothing for it but to get down onto the cess and pull the cords under the coaches. With vacuum brake thus not functioning we crawled into Wolverton and stopped with the handbrake. All very illegal but fortunately unnoticed.

By 1955 we were getting those wonderful BR Standard 2-6- 4 tanks with ample power to haul two coaches. I remember no 80040 in gleaming black livery lined out in the usual grey, yellow and red. The brakes and injector were a delight, when running bunker first you thanked Robin Riddles for having the bunker recessed thus giving an excellent view forward. The disadvantage of travelling bunker first is that you are peering at the track ahead, and when it comes to stopping you shut the regulator too quickly

Two views of a Railway Correspondence and Travel Society Special at Newport Pagnell on the 10 of October, 1954. The event was organised in conjunction with the Rambler's Association. From London, Elephant and Castle to Herne Hill, Tulse hill, Streatham Hill, Clapham Junction, Willesden Junction and Wembley Central. The RCTS took over the train at Cheddington travelling over the Aylesbury and Newport Pagnell branches and visited Wolverton Works. It returned to Bletchley where it became the 'Rambler's Special' once again. The Webb Coal tank was one of three survivors at this time. For most of her life she had worked the Aylesbury, Dunstable and Newport Pagnell branches.

H C Casserley

A Fairburn tank of Bletchley shed handles the 'South Midlands Rail Tour' of the Locomotive Club of Great Britain on the 17 October 1954. The train originated at Bedford (Midland) starting from the Hitchin Bay. It reached Bletchley along the Bedford branch, crossed over the flyover at Bletchley to call at Swanbourne Sidings on the branch to Oxford. It called at Northampton and Market Harborough before returning to its starting point, obviously calling at Newport Pagnell. After closure to passenger traffic this engine was responsible for the daily freight train.

Stephen Summerson

and then have to grope for the brake valve which is just behind you. But the controls are splendidly placed and I was rather pleased in the way in which I glided to a stop.

I had hoped that Fred Baldwin would have made a favourable comment. The engine just stood under the bridge carrying the Great Linford road and I had forgotten that the fire had by now nicely burned through and the safety valves lifted. Under the archway the noise was doubled. 'What did you want to stop under the arch for?' said Fred. Unfortunately I did just the same thing at Bradwell and got a withering glance from Fred. Fortunately he was too busy arguing with Ronnie to say much. For Fred

An interesting LCGB tour of 28 June behind 40421 2P of Kentish Town Shed ran from St Pancras via North London incline to the former LNWR main line visiting Rickmansworth, Aylesbury and Newport Pagnell branches seen here at Wolverton with the 'Crewe Special' Wolverton Works Shunter waiting in the background, on branch metals. On 28th June 1958 three of the Ramsbottom/Webb engines had been working at Wolverton from LNWR days finally withdrawn in 1959.

Stephen Summerson.

Splendidly photographed in September sunshine the South Bedfordshire Locomotive Club special 'The Cobbler' which started at Luton (Bute Street) ran Dunstable-Leighton Buzzard, along the main line to Wolverton then up the branch. This was on the 19 September 1964, a mark of the time was the diagonal stripe on the cab side which censured the locomotive as being forbidden to work under the electrification lines. A year later the prohibition would take effect as the main line was electrified.

Stephen Summerson.

'The Cobbler' at Great Linford station. The train was driven by branch line driver Fred Bateman.

Stephen Summerson.

supported Tottenham Hotspur, while Ronnie supported Arsenal, they were to engrossed to reprimand me. The Standards were beautiful machines and as the cab was over the bogie they rode like a coach.

We also had a variety of Stanier and Fairburn 2-6-4 tanks. They had been excellent machines in their prime but were well past that when they came to the branch in the mid- fifties. I remember one, no 42669 which had such worn valve gear that when you pulled up to mid-gear it was still cutting off at 50%.

I had four happy years driving on the branch, but in 1955 British Railways unsportingly closed Newport Shed and engines came down from Bletchley. Fred and Cyril left the branch and I was never asked on the footplate again. Worse still, in 1964 the branch closed and the track was lifted. I still have a number of photographs to remind me of an exciting and satisfying period of my life.'

Instructions for driving on the branch
Newport Pagnell to Wolverton Shut off steam at timber crossing to stop correctly in Great Linford station. Shut off steam at cemetery gates to stop nicely at Bradwell. On the return, shut off on crossing the culvert near the windmill to stop at Bradwell. The brake had to be kept on in the station owing to the gradient falling towards Wolverton. Shut off steam at the iron bridge to stop at Great Linford. Shut off steam at the fixed distant to stop in Newport Pagnell station. The gradient sloped towards the goods yard so care had to be taken on braking. Fortunately the buffer stops were 100 yards further on.

Guard Ron Webb of Newport Pagnell with an unknown driver of 7763 Coal Tank in LMS days.

Bob Berry Collection

Driver Fred Bateman with 41222 at Newport in the late fifties.

Fred Bateman

The late Dennis Mellor, fireman for 41222 at Newport in the late fifties.

Fred Bateman

Ken Langly and Driver Cyril Holman on 6601 ex-LNWR 2-4-2 tank at Newport Pagnell in 1953. A branch 2-4-2 tank was destroyed by fire in the Newport steam shed on 1 January, 1916.

F Cockman

The terminus of the Wolverton and Stony Stratford Tramway was at the station. The leisured pace of standing around for a photograph in the middle of the road is typical of those pre traffic Edwardian days. The station building is only twenty years old on this photograph. Entrance to a transport system diverse, confident and secure, not one that the population at large would have to endure.

Wolverton Archeological Society

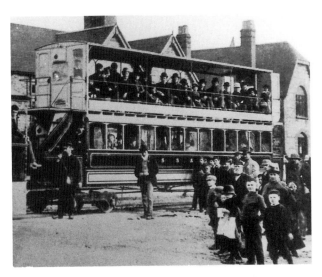

CHAPTER NINE

Wolverton & Stony Stratford Tramway

In view of the close association with the branch and the proposed tramway to Olney, it is of interest to view a more successful tramway. This was actually opened between the two towns of its name, not in standard gauge but in 3ft 6in gauge. It ran into the yard adjoining Wolverton station in effect providing a connection from Newport to Stony Stratford and Deanshanger.

The reason for the construction of the branch is to fulfil the same purpose as the branch; bringing workmen to the railway works and the close by printing works of McCorquodale's.

First proposal for the line appears in 1882 when it was incorporated as the Wolverton & Stony Stratford Tramway Co Ltd. This company seemed unable to generate the required capital and went into voluntary liquidation in 1883.

A Tramways Order was promoted by Frederick Charles Winby, a civil engineer and contractor on July 16, 1883. This was for 2 miles 54 chains. A single line of 4ft gauge from what was then the new Wolverton station to the north end of the High Street of Stony Stratford.

Although the Company was incorporated in September of the same year with authorised capital of £30,000 it lay dormant until 1886.

Bagnall saddle tank at Stony Stratford with one of the 100 seat workmen's cars.
The extended chimney is an obvious requirement for these high vehicles.

An association with the failed scheme of the Newport Pagnell – Olney
Tramway now took over the interests in this project. Charles Wilkinson of
Wilkinson & Co, building contractors for the proposed Newport – Olney
Tramway entered an estimate for the Stony Stratford line of £13,325,
accepting £2,000 in shares. They entered into contract with the company
in August 1888.

The line as authorised in 1883 received Board of Trade sanction on May
20, 1887 for 2 miles 15 chains single line and 40 chains double line. It was
built in 3ft 6in gauge rather the 4ft originally authorised.

Public passenger traffic began on May, 27, 1887 the same year of the
proposed construction of the Olney Tramway. From Wolverton station the
terminus was at the Barley Mow Inn, Stoney Stratford.

Wolverton & Stony Stratford train thought to be at Stony Stratford about 1909. Interesting reflection of the period that only the little girl would be excused the social decorum of always wearing a cap or hat out of doors.

Barry Davis Collection

Trains consisted of a tramway type steam locomotive hauling capacious double deck cars with covered tops. The charge of 2d (1p) was bound to seriously undercut the local horse omnibus services chargeing 6d (2½p) and hopelessly short of sufficient capacity. At its best it earned £2 to £3 per week whereas the Tramway was easily in receipt of £45 per week filled by hundreds of workmen. Weekly tickets of 1 shilling were issued entitling them to four journeys each day.

The Tramway Company was also interested in tapping the goods haulage potential for the area. This they did successfully with the LNWR. This was the initiative behind the promotion of the extension of the line from Stony Stratford to Deanshanger. A scheme was sanctioned by an order of July 19, 1887 for an extension of 2 miles 3 chains. The aim was a connection with the Britannia Ironworks of E & H Roberts, makers of Agricultural implements. By May 24 1888 the complete Tramway was in use from Wolverton to Deanshanger.

Regrettably this high point of the Tramway's life was very short lived as the Company became insolvent the following year and went into liquidation and was closed.

The Wolverton to Stony Stratford Tram stands on a passing loop in
Wolverton.

R G Westley

The original portion was, between Wolverton and Stony Stratford was
taken over in 1891 by a Bedford syndicate led by Sir Herbert Leon. They
reopened this section in November of that year. Now grandly proclaimed
as The Wolverton & Stony Stratford District New Tramway Co Ltd which
was incorporated in September 1893.

By 1919 the line was once more appearing rather neglected. Mid way
through the year the Company was placed into liquidation once more.
Like the Newport Pagnell branch the line was carrying a substantial
number of the large workforce, 700 daily. It seems odd that it should have
such a troubled existence, for with daily substantial numbers it had an
opportunity that many less fortunate branch lines would have dearly
wished for.

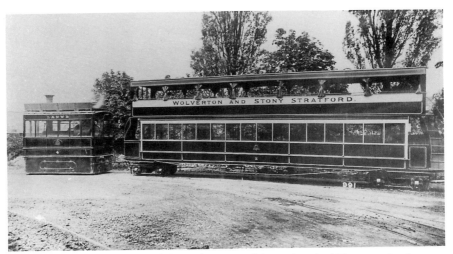

Locomotive and coach of the Wolverton and Stony Stratford Tramway. In the livery of the LNWR, this company took over the running of the Tramway in 1919 to save it from dereliction as it was heavily used by their workers. The coach is the product of the Midland Carriage & Wagon Co. at 44ft long and holding 100 passengers they were largest tramway coaches in use in this country. The locomotive was built by Thomas Green & Son.

LNWR Society.

In view of this and the goods service the LNWR took over the line in 1920. They relaid the rails in concrete and turned the locos and coaches out of their own paint shops in that superb livery lined carmine lake and ermine white, with the company's name and crest adorned.

This turned out to be a shining conclusion. The horse omnibus service so cruelly displaced in 1887 was to take its revenge in a different form. The age of the motor omnibus was ascendant. A new service was quicker and thus able to provide twelve return trips daily cutting deep into the patrons of the Tramway with its speed limit of 8 mph.

The inheritors of the LNWR undertakings, the LMSR considered electrifying the line as in many cities and towns but discounted this as unremunerative to the heavy cost. Finally in 1927 they managed to relieve themselves of the burden of the line to the Buckinghamshire County Council who simply removed the rails to reconstruct the road. This finally and unceremoniously completed the life of the Tramway in 1934.

Tramway locomotives

Engine	Builder	Year
Two	Krauss & Co, Munich	1887
Two	Thomas, Green & Son, Leeds	1887
One	Brush Electrical Engineering	1900
One Saddletank	W G Bagnell Ltd (for LNWR)	1921

Rolling Stock

Large d/d Covered	Midland Carriage & Wagon Co	1887
Five cars three large	?	1911?

Goods

Parcel vans and small wagons	Midland Carriage & Wagon Co	?
10 ton coal and coke trucks 24ft long	Midland Carriage & Wagon Co	?

For further details look in Railway Magazine August 1952 p547

Drawings of the station buildings at Newport Pagnell. In order to enclose them in these pages they are reduced to the modellers scale of 2mm to the foot. Should any reader wish to have them in a larger scale they can be obtained by inquiring with the publisher.

Fred Bateman

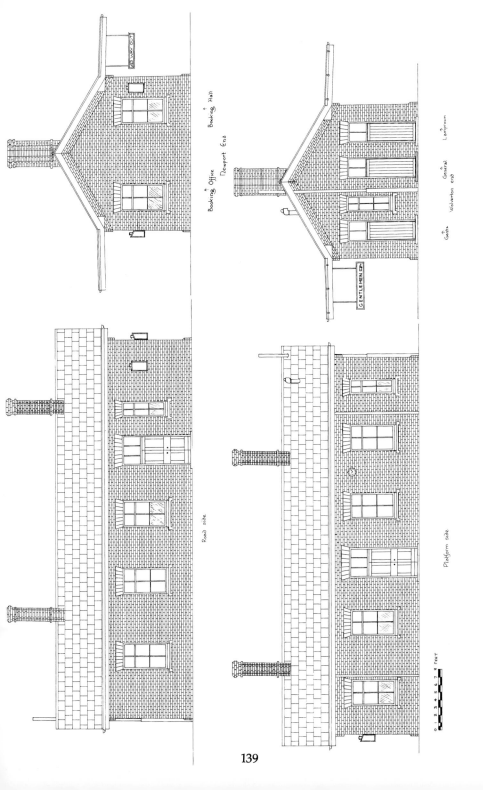

Booking Office ↑ Booking Hall ↑
Newport End

Gents ↑ Wolverton General ↑ Lamproom
End

Road side

Platform side

0 1 2 3 4 5 6 7 8 FEET

WAY OUT

GENTLEMEN

139

Acknowledgements

In compiling this history the author gratefully acknowledges the kind assistance of the following people who have generously supported his efforts.

Robert Ayres of the Wolverton & District Archeological Society, Fred Bateman, Ray Bailey, Bob Berry, Richard Casserley, Dr M J Chappell of the Newport Pagnell Historical Society, Mr J Coales, F G Cockman, Colin Stacey, Mr H Turvey, Mr R G Westley, Bill West, Staff of the County Records Office, Aylesbury.

Also the numerous photographers that have supplied from their collections, each credited with the photographs.

REFERENCES

The notes of Railway Historian, the late Geoffrey Webb.

Echoes of the Past, Newman Cole, Warren Dawson (Wolverton & District Archeological Society).

Wolverton Express.

Railway Magazine.

The Railwayman — Wolverton, Bill West.

In Railway Service, Arthur Grigg.

Index